MORAL PROBLEMS
AND
MENTAL HEALTH

MORAL PROBLEMS

AND

MENTAL HEALTH

RICHARD
EGENTER

PAUL
MATUSSEK

Translated by

MICHAEL BARRY

alba house DIVISION OF THE SOCIETY OF ST. PAUL
STATEN ISLAND, N.Y. 10314

First published in 1967 by
M. H. Gill & Son Ltd

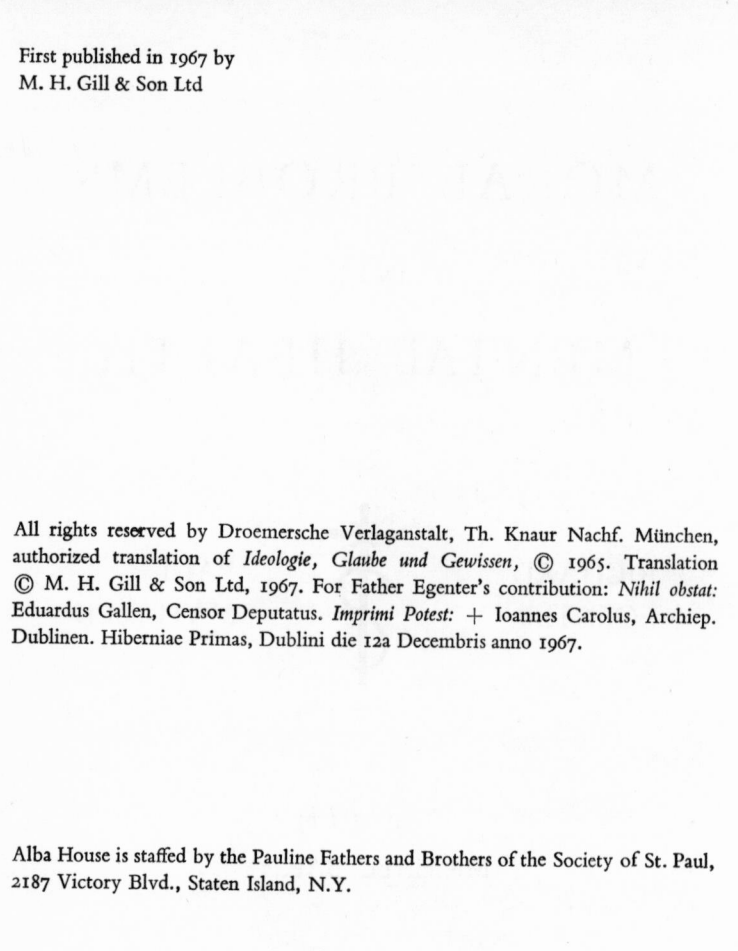

Alba House is staffed by the Pauline Fathers and Brothers of the Society of St. Paul, 2187 Victory Blvd., Staten Island, N.Y.

Printed and bound in the Republic of Ireland by
Cahill and Co. Limited, Dublin

CONTENTS

FOREWORD

Faith and morality, the formation of conscience and the making of responsible decisions based on conscience are among the central problems of human existence. Each individual attempts to solve these problems in his own way, independently of the psychological, social and religious influences he may have encountered in the course of his development.

It has always been the concern of theology to investigate the various ways in which decisions based on faith are reached, and hence also the various ways in which conscience may be formed. For theologians, too, faith is not just a matter of saying "Lord, Lord"; and not every decision of conscience is a genuine one. Pastoral theology is repeatedly coming up against problems which urgently require better and fuller answers. At the present time there is a particularly strong urge to find creative answers. The Church is once more on the move and is trying to express the old truths of revelation in a language which makes sense to the changed world of today. It is seeking a dialogue with the world, including the world of science, against which it has been too long on the defensive.

The dialogue with psychotherapy forms part of this confrontation with science. In some respects it is more important for the Church than the controversies with the purely natural sciences, which are concerned with the inanimate and the non-spiritual. These controversies could finish up in irreconcilable contradictions only when, as frequently enough happened, one or both of the parties overstepped their respective spheres of competence.

The confrontation of theology and psychotherapy, however, is another matter. Here it is a question of specifically human interests, the salvation and the healing of man. The boundaries of both disciplines overlap in man himself, and it is very hard to avoid trespassing. This makes it all the more important to enter into borderline discussions, so that both sides can find out how the other thinks and argues.

Such were the basic ideas which led us to conduct a discussion of these questions before students at the University of Munich during the winter semester of 1964/65. The interest aroused was so great that we decided to make excerpts of it available in book form. We decided, too, to preserve the conversational character to a very large extent, except where this did occasional violence to the demands of the written word. Hence the dialogue form, even though in some places it only provides a statement of the speaker's own position.

Psychotherapy is here taken to mean the type based on psychoanalysis, and thus psychotherapy and psychoanalysis are used synonymously. Strictly speaking, of course, this is wrong, because there are also other forms of psychotherapy which start from different assumptions. Theologically, however, psychoanalysis is the most interesting, largely because of its methodological advantages—though also, unfortunately, because of a number of theoretical formulations sometimes, though not always, attributable to Freud himself. It is also the form of psychotherapy which has come, for the layman (Christian or otherwise), to be considered as a book with seven seals. As a method, it has been the object of all sorts of prejudices, ranging from the attribution of quasi-magical powers to contemptuous dismissal, even though it now forms one of the indispensable elements of psychiatric research and treatment, and is also having an increasingly powerful bearing on the non-psychiatric disciplines of medical science.

For these reasons, therefore, Part I ("General Outlines") will be about questions which need to be clarified if ignorance and prejudice are to be broken down. The expert can pass over this chapter, but the layman will find a number of things which, we hope, will make it easier for him to get some grasp of what analytical psychotherapy is about.

Part II is a discussion of the misgivings of the Catholic moral theologian when confronted with analytical psychotherapy. These are here set out from the viewpoint of a morality expressed in specific denominational terms, though they do take up at least indirectly the misgivings which can be found among non-Catholics and non-Christians.

Part III is concerned with the ideas about faith and morality which a psychotherapist frequently meets among his patients. This refers not only to Catholics trying to conduct their lives on the basis of an ecclesiastically formulated moral code but also to non-Christians trying to attain to a genuine faith in whatever terms this may be formulated. To understand the questions and misgivings of such people the psychoanalyst can no longer withdraw to the most comfortable position—as was still possible for him at the beginning of the century—and explain away the whole religious phenomenon in psychological terms. He must take pains to understand concrete religious faith in its own terms and to appreciate the reasons for misgivings by making a close examination of religious doctrines in practice. In our opinion this is the only legitimate way, both practically and scientifically, of relating psychoanalytical experience to the truths of faith; and it makes no difference what terms these truths of faith are expressed in, whether Christian, atheist or other. Only in this way can the psychoanalyst do justice to a faith which his patient presents to him as a reality; and only in this way, too, will it be possible for him to point out the psychological factors, as well as the historical and sociological ones, which are of questionable value in the attainment of "true faith".

Ideology, belief and conscience, whatever forms they may take and to whatever extent each is respectively present, will

B

then turn out to be the unbroken thread which helps mark out the shifting borderline between the genuine and the spurious, the essential and the irrelevant, in each individual case. This was the reason for the title *Ideologie, Glaube und Gewissen* (Ideology, Belief and Conscience), even though these themes are dealt with only in Part III, and even there neither exclusively nor exhaustively. But that is where the main emphasis of the whole discussion lies.

Munich, June 1965   *Richard Egenter   Paul Matussek*

I

General Outlines

Father Egenter: It is very important for a priest to realize how much mischief he can cause if he takes it for granted that those entrusted to his care bear full moral responsibility for their every action. To take an example: a man of thirty, unmarried, comes to the priest and despondently confesses his frequent "sins of self-gratification". Objectively, sexual self-gratification is a grave offence against human sexuality, which, after all, is an expression of love for another person within the bond of matrimony. The priest, therefore, repeatedly exhorts the penitent to grit his teeth and fight on, and to seek strength for the struggle in prayer and frequent communion. And what happens? The young man becomes more and more despondent, and one day simply casts aside the intolerable burden of moral effort and religious practice. The fault lies with the priest. It should have occurred to him that the "vice" of self-gratification was out of keeping with the otherwise high moral standards of this young man. If he had realized this he would have been able to discern the torment of what was, in effect, a compulsive temptation. A priest with any experience in such matters would have seen clearly that this "vice" was the neurotic symptom of some other trouble which neither he nor the penitent himself could clearly recognize; and that, for the symptom to disappear, the cause would have to be removed first. The thing to do here would have been to refer the young man to a psychotherapist, and in the meantime tell him, in a kindly, pastoral way, not to pay too much attention to this disturbing symptom, which was not a sin for which he was

I

fully responsible, and instead to think much more about how merciful the Lord always was to sinful men. And he should have told him to go about his ordinary work to the best of his abilities and, above all, to try and be understanding, kind and helpful towards the people around him.

But a priest will be able to act in this way only if he knows something about the problems of depth psychology and if he expects psychotherapy to be really helpful.

At the same time, a priest in everyday life not infrequently comes up against misgivings and criticisms with regard to psychotherapeutic methods. He can hardly be expected to turn to a psychotherapist for help unless he is clear in his own mind about all the questions and doubts.

It would be best, then, to start with a number of informational questions, in the hope that they will make it easier to grasp the essential nature of psychotherapy as far as possible. This may help to put such misgivings on a rational basis and then to find out whether they will stand up to further examination.

The first question which occurs to us and to many laymen, and there is often disagreement here even among medical men, is:

1. Who needs psychotherapy?

Dr Matussek: This is an important question. There is a great deal of uncertainty here among the public in general, and not just among theologians. Many of the patients who have been referred to us want to know if they are already "so far gone" as to need treatment. For them, a psychotherapist is first and foremost a doctor for the "insane" and the mentally ill. Others, again, think that only weak-willed people need psychotherapy, and that normal people can master all their difficulties by force of will-power.

From the medical viewpoint your question could be answered, rather baldly and abstractly, like this: psychotherapy is needed by anyone who suffers from a psychic symptom, or a psychically conditioned physical symptom, which cannot be removed either by personal efforts or by medicaments. Examples would be people who suffer from constant depressions, or can make no contact with others even though they so badly want it and try desperately hard, those who compulsively—that is, senselessly—wash their hands forty or fifty times a day, or who are afraid to cross a road, or get into a lift, or those who develop manias, or have to keep on changing their partners or lovers. And also people who suffer from certain physical symptoms such as asthma, stomach ulcers, coronary embolism or a particular form of high blood-pressure.

E.: You say that psychotherapy is needed by anyone suffering from a psychic, or a psychically conditioned physical symptom which cannot be got over either by personal initiative or with the aid of medicaments. What I should like to ask is whether this should not also apply to people who *do* "get over" their complaints with the aid of medicaments? One has only to think of the misuse of stimulants and tranquillizers.

M.: You are perfectly right to point out that an ever increasing number of patients are taking pills to try and get rid of symptoms which really need a thorough psychotherapeutic examination. There is a very great danger that these people will become dependent on pills in the long run and overlook the fact that their symptoms are really signs of a need for inner re-orientation. More and more doctors are now taking this into account. All the same, it is important even here not to pour out the baby with the bath-water. There is a whole series of indications where the use of psychic drugs—with psychotic symptoms, for instance—can be extraordinarily beneficial, especially when combined with psychotherapy.

E.: I should like to put a more general question. Are not the people who need psychotherapy precisely those who do not realize the fact or refuse to admit it? By what signs can relatives or superiors tell whether psychotherapeutic treatment is necessary?

M.: Not all psychically-disturbed people think of their symptoms as needing treatment. A person suffering from eczema, blood-pressure or constant headaches feels that he is physically ill and expects the doctor to prescribe the appropriate physical remedy. Psychic disturbances, on the other hand, are often not recognized for what they are and may be perceived simply as natural reactions to particular environmental influences, such as overwork, a difficult employer or marital problems. The most drastic refusal of any sort of psychotherapeutic assistance will be found among sick people who need it most: by those who really are mentally ill. Neurotic and psychotic symptoms are qualitatively different from those of purely physical maladies.

There is also, of course, the fact that psychic abnormalities, including the so-called character neuroses, are not generally a danger to life like many physical maladies. The only exceptions here are the cases which lead to suicide. But in general anyone can live with his eccentricities, quirks and psychic abnormalities up to a ripe old age, and even, as with Hitler, be "successful". Life goes on functioning somehow or other, with and in spite of the difficulties—and, in some cases, very well indeed. Anything which cannot be put right, or which is considered purely negative, is readily ascribed to natural tendencies or to environment. Such people fail to notice that they are frustrating many possibilities of making their lives more rewarding and meaningful. Those who commit "psychical suicide" are generally not in a position to realize that they are doing so.

E.: Here is another question. Kurt Schneider once described psychopaths as people who suffer from themselves or cause those around them to suffer. It is often assumed that psychopaths differ from so-called neurotics in that their condition is something they are born with. In this case, sending them to a psychotherapist would not seem to promise much success. One might say that they have come into the world with twisted instruments and have to make do with them and learn to live with their difficulties. There can be no question here of calling hidden developmental disturbances and their causes into consciousness; their handicaps are perfectly apparent and the only possibility is to help them by means of "therapeutic" education and pastoral care.

M.: Psychopaths constitute a chapter of their own in psychopathology. Kurt Schneider's definition was excellent at the time, but now that more has come to be known about the psychology of neuroses it is necessary to tighten up the definition. Kurt Schneider's criterion, that the psychopath suffers from himself or makes other people around him suffer, is not sufficient to differentiate this condition from other groups of psychic illnesses. The same applies to neuroses and to certain forms of psychosis. You have only to think of the neurotic wife who is always going round with a duster and removing every speck of dust as soon as it settles. She can cause quite a lot of suffering for those around her. And this urge for cleanliness is often an agony for the woman herself.

Another thing which has been revised is the assumption that psychopathy is simply a hereditary, not an environmental, variation of psychic life. But the influence of certain hereditary factors is postulated even in the case of neurotics, and environmental factors do play a part in psychopathy. We are, in fact, still unable to separate the hereditary and the environmental in these disturbances—and even, for that matter, in the case of normal people. Environment and the sum of hereditary factors form an indivisible unity in any given individual.

So long as the situation remains obscure one will have to be careful in diagnosing psychopathy or in assuming that the psychopath is incurable. Perhaps the best way to illustrate the meaning of the term "psychopath" within the limits imposed here is to point to people who are of a chronic criminal disposition and show few, if any, signs of emotional attachment to their fellow men. For this reason they are also described as anethopaths.

In books of moral theology the notion of psychopathy is used much too schematically and its meaning is too often assumed to be definitely established. Many moral theologians use it as something on which to hang a number of misleading casuistries. It is not for pastoral theology to make such diagnoses. Whether it is possible to give much pastoral help to genuine psychopaths will always depend on the individual case.

E.: Your warning against hasty diagnoses by moral and pastoral theologians is quite right. On the other hand, is there not sometimes a tendency to conclude all too quickly that someone is a "case for the psychotherapist"? You have expressed the opinion that potential subjects for psychotherapy include not only a large proportion of people described as psychopaths but also, for example, people with coronary embolism or high blood-pressure. If all these people really stand in need of psychotherapy it would mean, surely, that half the human race, at least in our "civilized" countries, should have treatment? This suggests that psychotherapy will become the "fashionable thing"—as would appear, from all accounts, to have happened in the U.S.A.

M.: However offensive it may seem, it is hardly an exaggeration to say that half our population *could,* in fact, benefit from psychotherapeutic treatment. The general public, of course, inclines to the opinion that psychoanalysts are simply pushing up the figures to suit their own purposes. It would be advisable, perhaps, to look at the problem through non-medical eyes and try to grasp some of the reasons why it is often difficult for people to appreciate the indications for psychotherapeutic treatment.

From my own experience I would suggest that it is possible to divide the "material" for psychotherapeutic treatment very crudely into three groups, each of which arouses different lay reactions towards claims to the desirability or necessity of treatment. The relative numerical proportions of these groups have been very roughly assessed on the basis of statistics taken from the specialist literature. Since the incidence varies from one region to another I am keeping to the lower estimates rather than to the higher ones.

The first group is made up of sick people who would give even a non-medical observer the impression that the disturbances and symptoms in question are ones which the sufferer cannot get over without help and which should really be examined by a nerve specialist. Examples would be mental disorders, melancholia, a great variety of manias, extreme compulsive symptoms, depressions, morbid anxiety or certain sexual disturbances. It is estimated that these and equally conspicuous disturbances occur among at least ten per cent of the population at one period of life or another. Psychotherapy is definitely indicated, even if not as the only therapeutic measure.

The second group consists of those who have physical symptoms like asthma, eczema, certain cardiac and circulatory troubles, or stomach complaints. In these cases, however, not only the sufferers but even outsiders rarely get the impression that it might be advisable to consult a psychotherapist. The persons afflicted very understandably go first to the general practitioner or to a particular specialist.

Now, allowing for regional variations and different source material, the statistics given by these doctors show that approximately thirty to sixty per cent of people in a doctor's practice suffer from functional disturbances. The symptoms are of the sort for which no sufficient cause can be found in the organic condition but in which psychic components play a considerable part. In many cases psychotherapy can render very useful help indeed.

But only a small percentage of such patients ever get as far as psychotherapeutic treatment. The fact that doctors are insufficiently educated and enlightened on this subject, especially in Germany, is only partly responsible. To my mind, it is more often the attitude of the sufferers themselves which is decisive. They feel themselves to be ill only because of some cut-and-dried symptom, such as chronic headaches or stomach complaints, which they then blame for possible psychic symptoms such as tensions, depressions, moodiness or outbursts of anger. They demand—quite understandably—that the symptoms be removed immediately. But this is something which psychotherapy cannot do. Its business is not with the symptoms but with the underlying causes which are working themselves out in the patient's case-history. A certain length of time is needed if these levels of the personality are to be reached. The more undifferentiated the patient the more inclined he will be to dismiss any long-term treatment as "nonsense"—though usually he is very little bothered by the thought that his symptoms have been treated unsuccessfully for years on end with medicaments of all descriptions.

With this second group, in short, a symptom is assumed at once to be in need of medical help, and then perhaps of psychotherapy. But with the third and last group it is a question of disturbances which are generally not associated with medical or therapeutic treatment at all. The first reaction here is to think of natural disposition, particular environmental situations, normal developmental upsets or even, if such people are religious, a divinely imposed cross. These impressions are understandable when one reflects on the nature of the disturbances in this group, for whom the psychotherapist is definitely the right specialist to go to: serious inhibitions in human contacts, a chronic incapacity for giving or receiving love, a sense of the meaninglessness of existence, constant dissatisfaction or misery in married life, inadaptability in one's work, or the feeling that one is not loved or respected enough by one's children.

Hence that situation so familar to psychotherapists: a patient, living perhaps in a permanent inner conflict as regards his married life, tells his friends that he is undergoing psychoanalytical treatment. The reactions vary: amusement, astonishment, alarm or indignation. "Don't tell me you're going in for this nonsense too? They're only after your money. Your marriage is just as good as most other people's, if not better." What sort of answer can a man in his position make when he is asked why he is undergoing treatment? If he has physical symptoms as well he can afford to be fairly open about it all. But how is he ever to give an outsider, or even his closest relatives, a proper idea of his inmost needs, difficulties, thoughts and problems? Can he be expected to tell everyone that he finds himself unable to respond to others—his wife, his children, his friends, even society—and must learn what it means to accept and affirm and, even, to love?

To my mind, it is mainly on account of this last group that the public tends to resist psychotherapy and dismiss it as a fad. The number of people concerned is probably larger than in the other two groups. It is harder to give exact figures here because even the experts are not agreed about the criteria for diagnosing such disturbances. The dividing-line between normal and abnormal is somewhat fluid and depends on the point of view adopted. With the first group one could say that psychotherapy was necessary, but with this group it would be better to say that it could produce good results. But psychotherapy is now dealing with conditions which are generally described as "normal", and this may well be the reason why the public shows such resistance.

This resistance, it seems to me, is shared by the Church, or by a large proportion of the clergy. True enough, the disturbances I have described here are the sort of difficulties which people thought to be mainly in the province of the priest. The priest, in sermons or personal talks, or through his prayers and his proffering of supernatural aid, would try to bring people to see things in the light of faith and thus overcome them. Then psychotherapy suddenly makes its appearance and claims that many people must really be given psychotherapeutic treatment before the theologian can do anything useful at all.

Even though a certain amount of knowledge about the facts of psychoanalysis has gradually penetrated into the public awareness it will probably be many years yet before psychotherapy can be expertly carried out to a sufficient extent to be of real assistance to the patients. In Germany we have too few psychotherapists with a training in psychoanalysis. A few exceptions apart, they are found only in large or middle-sized towns. But they are so overworked that most people with physical disturbances of a psychic or psychogenic nature are forced to turn to a doctor who, lacking the necessary training, has taught himself a certain amount of psychotherapy. The fact, too, that the universities have for a very long time kept aloof from analytical psychotherapy, and to some extent still do, has had very unfortunate results. Institutes unattached to any university have had to try and fill in the present gaps in university teaching. In Germany, therefore, the danger that someone with serious neurotic or psychotic disturbances might not find the right doctor is so great that an analyst is hardly likely to take on a patient unless there are very serious indications.

E.: Even if one still entertains doubts about the percentage of those requiring psychotherapy one can none-the-less agree on the whole with the points you have brought up. All the same, there are still some misgivings from the pastoral point of view. Certainly there are cases where the work of a psychotherapist is needed before a priest can do anything with any prospect of success. But you yourself are envisaging cases where psychotherapy is not so much vital as useful. These are borderline cases, and while psychotherapeutic treatment might well be beneficial, the normal educational or pastoral methods would also seem to have good chances of success. A priest would hesitate to send such people straight to the psychotherapist.

What I should like to ask is this: is it not possible that too much canvassing for psychotherapy might tend to encourage hypochondria and an unwillingness to make a personal effort, and give people the idea that all the little aches and pains can be smoothed away by the psychotherapist? The danger is all the greater since people today allow themselves to be manipulated too much already by external agencies—the mass media, the "hidden persuaders", and so on.

M.: There is no doubt at all that a lot of patients do come to us with the wrong idea. They think that psychotherapy works on the same principle as a medication and they look on the practitioner as a sort of drug which, by means of various manipulations, can remove even serious personality troubles. What they lack is a willingness to give their own genuine co-operation and a determination to come to grips with themselves more thoroughly than before. Patients like this occasionally imagine that psychotherapy is a sort of hypnosis, and many of them even confuse the two. Anyone, then, who comes to us with these notions and thinks that all he needs to do is submit to influence without any effort on his own part is soon put right during the preliminary consultation.

But I will certainly grant you that psychotherapists have to reckon with exceptions of this sort. We are faced with much the same problem as the priest. He, too, will be aware—probably even more so—of the magical application of prayer, sacrifice and the sacraments. Unlike the psychotherapist, however, the priest can hardly determine in individual cases for what spiritual motives a parishioner is using the means made available by the Church. Often enough he will know people who, month after month, year after year, are always confessing the same sins and are trying just as persistently to combat them with the same instruments of grace. How is the priest to decide whether their internal attitude is one of genuine faith or whether their idea of the sacraments is a magical one based on habit? The psychotherapist, with the aid of his particular procedures, can unmask such evasive tactics comparatively quickly; but a priest cannot, and his counsels ("pray more frequently", "go to Mass more often") may even reinforce a spurious faith. This makes me think that the percentage of people who evade their problems is larger among believing Christians than in the consulting-rooms of the psychotherapists.

E.: It is probably no accident that the answer you give to a theologian's questions contains an important allusion to his pastoral practice. It is, in fact, important that a confessor should not give his instructions and exhortations simply as a "follow-up" to what his penitent has confessed. His business is to find out how far the confession springs from conscience and conviction—in other words, how far it is based on a genuine sense of guilt, on repentance, and on a willingness to amend. In the very short dialogue during a normal confession it will probably not be easy to recognize whether the self-accusations of the penitent are really being used unconsciously in an attempt to exonerate himself and thus evade his deeper moral and religious responsibilities. But assuming the confessor does not act as in the example you have given, and does not merely give the facile advice to multiply religious exercises but also tries to help the penitent to interiorize his religious practice more, he will be able in many cases to get nearer to the real roots of the penitent's moral and religious failure and make him come to grips with himself more effectively. But if, in spite of obvious goodwill on the penitent's part, this does not succeed, he will take it as a warning sign that there may be some serious neurotic disturbance present which calls for psychotherapeutic treatment.

M.: I ought to add something to the answer I gave when you asked whether hypochondria and unwillingness to make a personal effort might not lead many people to the psychotherapist. Although psychotherapy is not a comfortable, mechanical method, it is still based on an attitude towards individual human suffering which differs from that of many theologians. We are just as aware as the theologian that a life without danger, suffering and failure is not possible, and even psychotherapy demands certain sacrifices if a person is to be made better able to cope with his limitations and sufferings. Where we differ from the theologian is in the judgment we form about suffering in particular cases.

We do not recognize every suffering as God's will, a blessing, a share in Christ's cross, or atonement for one's own or other people's sins. We are also familiar with people who, for unconscious reasons, simply have to suffer in order to obtain a certain measure of gratification. A theologian's methods do not enable him to discern motives of this sort, and there is even a danger that he may encourage these motives without realizing it. Take the example of a mother who is constantly suffering from her husband, children and household, although what she has to put up with is by no means worse or more taxing than in other families. Mothers with this urge to suffer may well be identifying themselves in spirit with Mary, Mother of Sorrows; but they can wreck marriages and seriously retard their children's development, without an outsider being in a position to recognize the underlying mechanisms. Patients with disturbances of this sort are frequently resistant to therapy; in other words, they break off analysis before they are really cured. Subjective suffering has become such an essential factor in their spiritual economy that a life free of symptoms seems quite impossible to them.

E.: As a theologian I should be interested to know to what extent even people with religious problems should seek therapy. In rather simpler terms, it is obvious that psychic troubles can also manifest themselves in religious life. For example, some people are overcome by fear in closed and crowded places, and this may well be brought on by a visit to a full church on Sunday. I am not concerned so much with this particular point as with a more specific question: to what extent can religious life as such give rise to psychic disturbances?

M.: Strictly speaking, no isolated department of life can ever be the reason for a neurosis. A neurosis will be conditioned by many factors together and must be traced ultimately to a whole set of factors, both genetic—hence hereditary—and biographical. As a result, many things which were said in the early days of psychoanalysis, such as that neuroses could be blamed on religion in general, have turned out to be false.

All the same, forms of religious behaviour can play a part in the appearance of neurotic symptoms among certain individuals. This can be seen from the cases where neurotic symptoms disappear or become less pronounced as soon as particular forms of religious thought and behaviour are abandoned. For example, a person may stop going to church, or give up praying, or turn away from his particular denomination altogether. When transformations of this sort take place during the course of analysis theologians often take it as proof that the psychoanalytical process is destructive of faith. But this would be to forget that analytical treatment sometimes produces the opposite effect and turns a non-Christian life into a Christian one. What is more, when people make judgments like this they are simply equating particular external religious forms with religion, or Christianity, as such.

The conceptually fixed ideas about God in a person's life, as well as the denominational or non-denominational patterns of behaviour which result from them, are always dependent on a series of biographical factors. Thus, for some people, the sole proof for the truth of a religion is the fact that that was what their parents believed. But for adults such dependence is not sufficient motive for a truly personal religious conviction. The Christian churches are fully aware of this and are acting accordingly whenever they carry out missionary work among people of different faiths and try to draw them away from the beliefs they have learnt from their fathers.

This principle also applies the other way round. When young people want to break loose from their parents and attain personal independence they turn away from their childhood faith. This protest is no more a valid decision based on an appraisal of the facts than was the uncritical adoption of the parental faith; but as a concrete attempt to adopt a personal attitude towards religion it should be taken with due seriousness.

My reason for this example was simply to show that an individual's religious ideas can contribute to the development of neurotic symptoms. This means, of course, that these symptoms can disappear when the religious ideas are changed. A familiar example, perhaps, is that of priests who lose a whole lot of their symptoms, such as depressions, compulsions or ideological attitudes, when they abandon their profession. This is not to say that the change of symptoms offers a guarantee that these people will now become mature personalities in the psychoanalytical sense. But it does show that symptoms can undergo a change when particular religious ideas are abandoned.

E.: Another question, which perhaps ties up with the last one: are there psychic disturbances which manifest themselves primarily or even exclusively in the religious sphere? I am thinking, say, of people who seem perfectly normal and are conspicuous only for their scrupulous attitude in the confessional. They go frequently to confession, but are overcome by scruples of all descriptions. For them the acknowledgment of guilt amounts practically to an endless obligation which they vainly try to fulfil by constantly renewing their examinations of conscience and repeatedly attempting to make fuller confessions.

M.: There are, perhaps, two aspects to be distinguished here: one subjective, and the other objective. It is subjectively possible that a person may go for psychotherapeutic treatment simply on account of certain peculiarities in his religious life, such as scrupulosity in confession or some tormenting crisis of faith. But these cases are probably extremely rare, and they cannot obscure the fact that, objectively, there are no disturbances in the religious sphere which are without repercussions in the other departments of a person's life. Briefly and simply, everything is tied up together. There is no such thing as a religious problem in isolation, any more than there are physical troubles of a neurotic nature which are not bound up with the person's relation to his environment.

The example you gave is a special case of the principle I have just referred to. What peculiarities and symptoms make a patient decide to have treatment? The symptoms of which a person is conscious are not co-extensive with the disturbances which are objectively present. In the case of a religious person there can be a number of very peculiar situations. For example, the only thing which troubles him may be his dislike of going to church or his scruples in confession, yet he may be quite blind to what he really feels about his wife or children. In therapy it can often be a considerable time before such people are in a position to admit their "lovelessness" and put it right.

This example also shows one of the many effects of psychoanalysis which is generally overlooked. It is quite often assumed that the analyst gets straight to work on the conscious symptom and removes it, just like a surgeon who, when dealing with a stomach ulcer, simply operates on the stomach without troubling about all the other organs. But with psychotherapy, which has to do with psychic patterns, this is never the case. Moodiness, fear of the dark, scruples, manias, nervousness, cardiac sensations—these are just part of a ramified structure. Hence treatment always consists of making the patient aware of many peculiarities which he was previously unable to experience for what they really were.

It is quite understandable, then, that people who have been aware of their problems predominantly in a religious context should harbour a number of prejudices and aversions to psychotherapy. They feel unconsciously that there is something more behind their symptoms than merely a passing crisis of faith or particular scruples in confession. But this "something more", which they obscurely sense but are unwilling to face up to, is a cherished, and immature, idea about themselves and the world which they do not want to renounce.

For this reason I can well imagine that people with particular religious problems might benefit from expert psychoanalysis. In any case, it does not seem to me entirely satisfactory to try and combat aridity, narrow-mindedness, uncharitableness or certain constantly recurring sins simply by religious means, without at least asking whether there might not be underlying peculiarities of personality which theological means cannot, in fact, remove.

E.: This leads to another question. Does man's response to divine revelation—in other words, faith and a religious and moral life inspired by faith—form a proper object for psychoanalytic investigation? Or is this a sphere in which divine grace alone should be the therapist? If faith and life lived in faith are taken in the strict Christian sense as a salvation event or as a personal inclusion in this salvation event, and not just as another human factor to be reckoned with, then it can well be asked whether the competence here belongs to psychotherapy or to what theologians call the *gratia medicinalis*, the grace of God's compassion. In so far as the latter is the case a priest should not hand over his "patients" to the psychotherapist.

M.: In practice, a priest would hardly send a "patient" to the psychotherapist as a method of checking up on what faith or salvation really mean to him. But if someone is under psycho-analytical treatment for any of the symptoms referred to earlier then the analysis will also include all questions connected with his faith. The salvation event you spoke of does not take place in a vacuum but always in a particular individual according to his character and personal history. It is impossible to keep his faith in a separate compartment. To try and do so, in fact, would be in actual contradiction to Christian teaching, since according to this teaching every personal faith is expressed through the actual conditions of real life, and it would be un-christian to postulate a faith without the "flesh". If a person's faith is mature and genuine it will be deepened by analysis, not destroyed. But if his faith is less than genuine, psycho-analytical treatment will be of help in so far as it can clear the ground for genuine faith. Religious ideas can all too easily be used as a cover-up for deeper personal characteristics, and this in itself is a hindrance to personal fulfilment even in the religious sense.

Furthermore, the expression *gratia medicinalis* you have just employed seems to me extremely dangerous when it comes to teaching and explaining religion. It could encourage the idea that God is accustomed to by-pass nature and intervene directly. I have come across not a few patients who pray for

God's help in this way and try to mobilize it for tensions, nerves, anxiety and even serious illnesses. They will not accept even medical aid, let alone psychotherapy, and talk of the greater efficacy of grace.

E.: Naturally the technical term *gratia medicinalis* belongs neither in the pulpit nor in the catechism class. But the theological reality behind it must be defended. A believing Christian will, and may legitimately, reckon with God's intervention in the world of nature. When that happens it will not, of course, be for the sake of natural self-fulfilment or psychic health, and most certainly not in order to save anyone from the moral and religious exertion required of him, but for the sake of salvation—in other words, for a supernatural purpose. However much the Church upholds the principle, it will always insist on genuine personal effort and never sanction the idea that this can be replaced by mere prayer for the intervention of divine grace. Prayer and personal exertion belong together.

2. What happens in psychotherapy?

E.: Suppose, now, someone comes to you, perhaps a person suffering from a stomach ulcer or acute nervousness, or a theology student with morbid scruples—what will happen during a course of analytical psychotherapy?

M.: Before the psychoanalyst makes any decision as to whether analytical psychotherapy is indicated, or even feasible, in a particular case he will carry out a trial analysis of about ten to twenty sessions. This not only helps the practitioner find his bearings but also enables the patient to get to know the analyst and find out whether he is a person with whom he is prepared to co-operate over an extended period of time.

The patient must discover whether he can open up to this doctor in such a way that he will even be able to bring to consciousness those aspects of his past life which combined to bring about the disturbance. After this trial run many patients have the impression that they cannot change their analyst because they think he might resent it. Technically, a negative decision on the patient's part should not worry the analyst, for he himself knows how much depends on complete trust, a trust which must be much greater than any placed in a father confessor.

On the other hand, the analyst also has a chance of getting to know the patient better. He can form a rough picture of the extent of the symptoms and assess the patient's willingness to co-operate seriously. This willingness is shown in the first place by whether the patient honestly observes the agreement made at the beginning of the treatment. Apart from a few technical details (number of sessions a week, the amount of the fee, etc.) the main point of the agreement is that the patient should express anything which may happen to come into his mind. This should be done without any reservations. Everyone knows, of course, that the patient in most cases lies on the couch with the analyst behind him. The only purpose of this "seating arrangement", which is not equally desirable in every instance, is to ensure that the patient is as relaxed as possible and can gradually give freer and freer expression to his thoughts. What Freud understood by free association is not present from the very outset. Only as time goes by does the patient learn to express even things which seem banal, stupid, indecent or irrelevant. He then comes to see them increasingly as little things which crop up during the course of a normal conversation. As time goes on the ideas will occur to him more and more freely.

E.: What you have just said is very welcome, because it must be reassuring for the "patient" to know that going to see a psychotherapist does not imply an irreversible decision to undergo treatment at his hands. It is obvious even to the layman that a long and delicate process like therapeutic analysis can only be carried out by means of an extremely personal dialogue. Both sides have to be sure that they are really tuned-in to one another, and this is something which cannot be taken for granted, however willing the patient or however eminent the psychotherapist. It would be a good thing if this could be pointed out quite clearly whenever a person comes to a psychotherapist, for it would eliminate at least *one* major source of possible failures.

But you also spoke of an agreement by which the patient undertakes to make known unreservedly everything that comes into his mind, and this raises a number of doubts from the ethical point of view. Before I go into that, though, I should like to ask you to describe in a little more detail the actual *course* of psychotherapeutical treatment. Three questions suggest themselves.

The first is this: does psychotherapeutic treatment always involve a lengthy depth analysis, or does the psychotherapist also have other effective methods —shorter and less expensive — of removing neurotic or even psychotic impediments?

M.: The question of the various types of psychotherapy strikes me as very important. Even the medically informed public tends to ignore the differences between them. Conversations for the purpose of giving consolation or encouragement, the bringing into the open of conflicts, the interpretation of dreams in one form or another, methods based on suggestion, processes involving depth psychology—these and a number of other things are all lumped together as psychotherapy, and because they all have a therapeutic effect it is assumed that one and the same process is responsible. This view is very widespread, and it is rather like referring to the chemical treatment of illness simply as chemotherapy without making any distinction between, say, penicillin and aspirin. Psychotherapeutic methods can take very different forms, depending on the patient's problem or on the proposed method of tackling it. To give a more detailed account of these differences would go far beyond the limits of this discussion, which is being confined to psychoanalytical psychotherapy.

As to the length of treatment, this is governed by a comparatively external criterion. Five or six years may sometimes be needed for psychotherapeutic treatment concerned merely with problems very near the level of consciousness; while a course of analytical psychotherapy in the strict sense might be over in two or three years. Only one thing can be said about the length—a course of psychotherapy lasting only six months or a year can never be analytical therapy, because within such a period the analytical process could never reach down to the depths where the changes are needed if the symptoms are to be permanently cleared up. This does not mean that the shorter procedures aimed rather at conscious conflicts are valueless. These existed before the analytical era in psychotherapy, and even today they have a big part to play in neurological consultations; with the aid of psychic drugs they help make up for the large gap created by the shortage of doctors with an analytical training.

When it comes to the individual case one has always to weigh up a number of factors before deciding whether psychotherapy is indicated, and if so, which sort. Here the illness itself is only one factor among many. Intelligence, social position, the degree of psychic differentiation, professional standing, powers of judgment, the grievousness of the symptoms, age, willingness to submit to treatment, and possibly even the co-operation of people close to the patient can all be very important.

The last of these factors has recently proved to be highly important; before the efficacy of psychotherapy was scientifically investigated it had long tended to be overlooked. Thus, in an extreme case, a course of treatment based on this view may—to take an example—make it seem as though it was the parents who were being more intensively examined than their eighteen-year-old son who lived at home with them, but who did not seem to be "coming on", because of serious developmental troubles, and had been sent to the psychotherapist. There is no question, in this case, of leaving the young man untreated; but more importance has come to be attached—as far as circumstances permit—to the removal of pathogenic factors in the immediate environment. The same principle can also apply to married couples. The relatives of someone with psychic troubles are often very touchy when we advise them to undergo therapy. "It's not we who aren't all there, it's our child." "If my husband's gone off his head then it's nothing to do with *me*. I'd be quite different if he wasn't so queer." There are very few parents, among psychotics at least, who see things as clearly as the mother who listened to my suggestion and, after a few misgivings, said: "I find it very hard, but I can see that I ought to be treated too. There's no point delousing my daughter twice a week and then sending her back to sleep in a louse-ridden bed."

E.: Now for my second question. What, in very crude and schematic terms, is the procedure followed during therapeutic analysis? The uninitiated often find this rather shrouded in mystery. They have heard of dream analysis, free association, narco-analysis, resistance, transference and counter-transference, release of repressed energies, and also of psychagogy. These concepts and catchwords which have filtered through from the discussions among the experts normally offer no clear picture of what goes on during therapeutic analysis. Even a schematic account of what might happen during a sort of "text-book" analysis might help to remove a lot of reservations, objections and vague ideas,

M.: You are quite right to point out that this question can only be answered schematically. The external features are as diverse as the different causes of neurotic or psychotic symptoms. Thus, whether the patient sits or lies, has five sessions a week or only one, and talks a lot or very little; whether his dreams are long or short, frightening or liberating, and whether the analyst interprets them frequently, occasionally or not at all; and whether the analyst expresses no opinion whatsoever, or throws in the occasional argument, or even makes suggestions—all these are external features, the meaning behind which can only be understood from a detailed familiarity with the life and symptoms of the patient and the training the analyst has received.

But the part of the process which is going on behind this array of different externals can perhaps be summed up in rather simple terms as follows. At the beginning of treatment the patient still talks about himself and his life as he might to a good friend; but after a time he starts to realize other facts about his internal life and his past which previously he had seen either not at all or in a very different light. He will suddenly remember experiences which had seemed to him long over and done with. In this process an important part is played by dreams. The analyst does not provide the patient with ready-made interpretations straight out of the book, as is often assumed. In fact, the patient himself usually begins to get the feeling that these images are not just froth, or the aftermath of an indigestible meal, but the pictorial expression of personal experience and of attitudes towards himself and the world around him. The degree to which he becomes able to accept and interpret such pieces of information depends on the stage of analysis reached. In this process the analyst remains to all appearances nothing more than a quiet and attentive listener, occasionally asking questions or putting forward interpretations; what he is really doing is co-operating with the patient in order to help him make the first steps into the unconscious. Without him the patient would never venture into the depths of his own personality, or perhaps not recognize what he sees there as aspects of his own life which had previously been suppressed and pushed aside so that they could only be "lived out" in symptoms.

To illustrate this by another example we could go back to the woman who is always doing the rounds with her duster, unable to bear the sight of any mess. For her, the really important thing in family life is a clean home, and everything else has to take second place. A peculiarity like this will not necessarily strike people as anything abnormal, and if it is taken as typical of countless other peculiarities with some psychological significance the following pattern will emerge.

A woman like this will never, or only under very special circumstances, come for treatment for behaviour of this sort. It is much more likely that psychotherapeutic treatment will be resorted to on account of certain physical symptoms. During the first weeks of analysis the patient will come out with every imaginable thing about her life and her sufferings, but she will never refer to this one peculiarity. It never even occurs to her. And if she does happen to refer to it, then it will not be because she is convinced that it is the expression of a personal problem. This behaviour will easily be accounted for as a natural reaction to her surroundings. "The children are always bringing such a lot of dirt into the house." "You have to keep at it, or the place would soon become a pig-sty." "My husband's none too particular about tidiness either." But all this time she may have been bringing to mind a whole lot of past experiences or present attitudes which she found very hard indeed to talk about. She may even have the impression that she now sees her shortcomings and is "confessing" them. Objectively the content of these "confessions" may well be much more serious (perhaps an abortion, an adultery, a theft, and so on) than the mere fact that she finds her dusting activities to be personally gratifying.

It is important to be clear about this, because people often confuse psychoanalysis with confession and think that the difficulty in psychoanalytical treatment is talking about objectively "offensive" experiences or actions. The real difficulties, however, are felt with the problems which one thinks of as mainly unpleasant, embarrassing and shameful. But this is what psychoanalysis is about: its only concern is for things which are really relevant to the course of a person's life and development, and for things which are unique to that person alone. As this process starts to go down deeper it may well happen that our patient suddenly realizes that she is cleaning up the dirt not for the sake of the dirt itself but in order to gratify her own urges. At first this is as far as she will go. After all the things she has been revealing up to now this is no more than the next step towards her unconscious. It now becomes possible for her to take in herself and her environment in a wider sweep than before, though this ability will not grow evenly and steadily but will be constantly interrupted and endangered by impulses to hold tight to the old familiar way of seeing herself. Thus, when the woman realizes that her urge for cleanliness is the reflection of an internal rather than of an external necessity, she may well remain content with this and abruptly suggest that the analyst should tell her where these impulses can possibly come from. There is here what is called a resistance—not in the question itself, which might well be a perfectly legitimate one, but in the attitude behind it. She is resisting further self-knowledge, or, to put it more accurately, she is resisting the attempt to re-direct impulses which once had a meaning when they were formed in early childhood but which are now only helping to keep her symptoms in being and restricting her freedom to respond fully to the world around her.

E.: The outline you have given of these important happenings in the process of analysis will probably be filled in during the course of our discussion; but it prompts a non-expert to ask what happens at the end of a successful course of psychotherapy. When can the psychotherapist say "I think the time has come to break off"?

M.: The end of analytical treatment is determined mainly by the patient. When not only the symptoms for which he was being treated but also a number of further difficulties have been cleared up he will start thinking about breaking off analysis and will discuss his intention with the analyst. Whether the analyst has the same impression as the patient depends on a series of factors which were playing a part when treatment was taken up and the indications established. Generally speaking he lets himself be guided by pragmatic rather than by theoretical considerations. He will ask, for example, whether the patient will now be able on the whole to cope with his life and situation in a more mature way. This pragmatic standpoint is based simply on the medical indications, which is not the same thing as the theoretical consideration that the therapeutic effects on the patient might be greater if psychoanalysis were intensified or prolonged.

There is perhaps a parallel here with the attitude of the priest. He, too, may know that a daily dialogue with God in meditation and prayer might well be fruitful for personal development. All the same, he will very seldom give this advice, even though, in our externalized welfare society with its increasing problems of how to fill up spare time, meditation and prayer could have a very beneficial internalizing effect.

II

A Moral Theologian's Queries

Fr Egenter: Your survey of the psychoanalytical process makes it clear that its success depends entirely on the extent to which it manages to bring to consciousness things which have been suppressed or inhibited in the course of psychic development and to integrate them into the patient's personal life. With serious psychic disturbances, or physical ones conditioned by psychic factors, this is certainly a legitimate end. But a number of misgivings make themselves felt in this connection and a discussion of them may help to clarify matters.

1. Doubts about the method of bringing to consciousness

E.: In order to bring suppressed psychic factors to consciousness the psychotherapist requires his patient to express everything which comes into his mind at a particular moment. From the Church's viewpoint objections have been raised against free association as a method, and the most notable instance is surely Pope Pius XII's discourse of 13 April 1953.

It is well known that a papal address of this sort cannot lay claim to infallibility, particularly since the questions here touched upon are not immediately referred to in divine revelation; it is a matter rather of assessing psychological or medical discoveries and practices in the light of natural moral law. Thus, in this case, the Pope was dependent on the information at his disposal, and it is possible, and even necessary, to enquire whether the Pope's information was accurate and complete when he made his pronouncement. It may also be asked whether, since that time, there have been any scientific advances which demand a more differentiated judgment on the part of moral theologians. Therefore, I am not quoting the Pope's words in order to stifle discussion, but only to bring out the questions which need to be cleared up; the Pope's words do, after all, represent a definite position of the Church, and although they cannot claim infallibility they carry incomparably more weight than the private opinion of an individual moral theologian. An authoritative pronouncement like this must be taken seriously if the matter is to be explained in a way which satisfies the demands of intellect and conscience alike. Now for what the Pope had to say.

a) May one allow everything to come freely to mind?

E.: The first question is whether it is permissible to allow everything to come to mind during the course of free association. Pius XII, who in any case was speaking only of "certain forms of psychoanalysis", confined himself to the sexual sphere. To start with, he doubted whether disturbances in this sphere could be removed by simply calling them into consciousness. And he went on to deny that it was permissible to allow free rein to everything which occurs to one in regard to sex. "Indeed it cannot be described as morally permissible to call to consciousness, or make psychically present, every sexual idea, feeling and experience which is slumbering in the unconscious and in the memory. If one gives ear to the protests raised by human and Christian dignity, can one venture to assert that this process contains no moral danger either at that moment or later on? The therapeutic necessity of this unrestrained disclosure has been asserted, but up to now by no means proved."

It might be easier to clarify this point if the question is not confined to the sexual sphere. Instead one might ask: is it not contrary to personal dignity simply to abandon oneself to one's associations? This would include stirrings of hatred or aggression towards our fellow men, impulses to blasphemy in religious matters, and so on.

Dr Matussek: As far as this danger is concerned the way you describe the process suggests a number of mistaken ideas, which are certainly very widely held. Your concern is obviously based on the assumption that the patient is able to think about and express his unconscious ideas and emotions, just like that. But this is very far from being the case. Freud chose the expression "unconscious", and this itself should have made the critics of psychoanalysis more cautious. It means precisely that the patient is *not* able to approach all the contents of his psychic life freely and unrestrainedly.

Since these ideas are strictly unconscious they can be made conscious only by means of a particular method, namely psychoanalysis; and among them there will occasionally be morally objectionable stirrings. And their moral objectionableness is often the reason why they have been kept from consciousness. To that extent there is a moral problem here. The patient senses this, too, as can be seen from his reluctance to put an end to the laboriously built up repressions which appear in certain characteristic modes of behaviour and to come to grips with the objectionable ideas which lie below the surface. The result is disgust and resistance. The psychoanalyst's job is to recognize this resistance and gradually break it down, not to reinforce the inhibitions, as the moral theologians would evidently wish.

This apparent antithesis between the "moral" conception of the moral theologians and the "immoral" conception of the psychoanalysts will be resolved when one understands the development and dynamics of what the psychoanalyst calls the unconscious. The ideas which the Ego, or responsible consciousness, finds objectionable are mainly ones which were acquired in childhood. The repressions which took place at that time were not based on mature moral decisions but on combinations of family factors which led to a "compulsion" to repress things. In so far as these repressions have not led to complications in the course of subsequent character formation, then a person will not, unless under psychoanalysis, be concerned with his unconscious. But when the dynamics have been such as to produce serious character defects or neurotic symptoms in later life, then he will have to try and face up to a number of ideas which have formed during development—and this is only part of the total process. If the responsible Ego is to develop and the person to grow to full maturity, then the concealed aspects of the personality will have to be confronted. And it is surely part of moral consciousness to learn to realize that one is not quite as moral as one may have been making oneself out to be.

Such conceptions of the significance of the unconscious should not lead anyone to suppose that the only things expressed during analytical treatment belong to the unconscious. The unconscious in this mythical sense does not exist. It is always bound up with conscious thoughts, or at least with thoughts which can easily be brought to consciousness, and by far the greater part of all that is expressed belongs in this category. And here too there will be attitudes, thoughts, feelings and wishes which in the theological sense are immoral. Thus there is no need to go down into the unconscious in order to find what a moral theologian would call immoral, and this applies even to people who generally think of themselves as devout or religious. These people, too, can get worked up about trifling faults in their neighbours, or

C

think themselves better than others, or abuse their authority. But according to the psychoanalytical view these and similar "immoral"attitudes and feelings will not be removed during therapy by keeping them secret. The patient should express them and come to terms with them in the analyst's presence.

This aspect of the analytical process might perhaps be described as the confrontation of internal and external, of what one experiences in oneself and what one communicates to others. This implies a difference between what I experience only in myself and what I give others to see and think about me. This releasing of internal experience to another person, in this case to the analyst, is very similar to the process of uncovering so-called unconscious material, and is every bit as important. It creates a relationship in which it becomes possible to penetrate into things previously excluded from conscious experience.

It seems to me as though the Pope, or his advisers, were confusing the antithesis between internal and external with the antithesis between conscious and unconscious. His misgivings appear to be concerned mainly with the communication of thoughts which are near to consciousness and can easily be elicited. But surely the Pope and the moral theologians did not really think that "immoral" ideas which remain unexpressed and unacknowledged in the course of therapy are somehow more moral than those which are expressed and confided to another person. The front against which psychoanalysis sets its face in theory and practice alike is not morality itself but a morality which is externalized, and hence sterile.

E.: The last few points you have raised touch upon a question which has still to be asked—the extent to which it is permissible to communicate to the therapist whatever comes to mind. I will be quite clear about this from the very start and say that it is ethically more desirable to refrain from communicating without sufficient reason objectionable thoughts such as hatred towards a third party, and to endeavour inwardly to reject such thoughts. The question is simply whether the end proposed by analysis does, in fact, provide such a sufficient reason for communicating thoughts which are morally negative in content. I would, myself, say that it does, although we shall see that Pius XII entertained misgivings in certain cases.

The Pope's first concern was about the things themselves which come to mind, in other words, what the patient allows to go on in his consciousness. He may either give free rein to his ideas and associations, or he may try to dissociate himself inwardly from certain ideas and turn away from them by directing his attention to other objects. The Pope's line of thought here was that of a pastor concerned with concrete questions rather than that of a theoretical scientist. Given the human condition, he considered it dangerous to adopt a purely passive attitude to the flow of consciousness, in other words, to let everything come into one's mind without intervening critically. And it would probably amount to the same thing whether these thoughts are previously repressed matter which can only be brought to consciousness with great difficulty or whether they are imaginings or stirrings which are always liable to come to the surface at any moment.

These imaginings and stirrings are often charged with emotion, and our emotions "tend to spread throughout the conscious mind". Once they have taken hold of the conscious the new psychic content which has been allowed admission will be coloured mainly by the emotions and impulses aroused. Thus, when the imagination is allowed to go its way without control or critical discernment a process is set up which can easily take a morally reprehensible direction. A theologian will be thinking here, of course, of the "disordered concupiscence" resulting from original sin. As experience shows, it is by no means out of the question that complete passivity towards what comes into one's mind may lead to a painful churning out, say, of sexual or aggressive thoughts accompanied by violent desire, especially when the patient somehow senses that this is just what the therapist is waiting for, either because it fits in with his theories or because he has not kept his human emotions sufficiently under control during transference and counter-transference, which is often a tricky situation. Conversation with an analyst (as with a priest, for that matter) can very easily descend into the all-too-human, a fact you will be as little concerned to deny as you are to condone. To this extent one can appreciate why the Pope urged upon patients and psychoanalysts alike the need of responsibility and spiritual discipline. But I am sure that it does not imply any condemnation of psychotherapeutic procedure if correctly carried out.

But correct procedure is your whole concern, and it seems to me that the moral theologian need raise no further doubts on this score. Moral misgivings recede if psychotherapist and patient "persevere faithfully with analysis", that is, if the patient honestly and openly expresses his associations and the feelings these arouse, and if the psychotherapist pays close attention to what is said and tries in this way to learn more about his patient's internal life. To recount what comes to mind is not necessarily to affirm it; as an act it is indifferent, though not always without moral dangers. After all, when the Christian allows his sins to come to mind when examining his conscience before confession, his intention is not to gloat over them (a very human failing which can certainly occur) but to receive absolution; in the same way a patient will express his thoughts during analysis for the very good and important purpose of being cured. All the same, there are perhaps a number of cases which still give rise to doubts, and I should like to come back to these later.

b) *May one express everything which comes to mind?*

E.: I should like to bring forward another objection which the Pope raised against the psychoanalytic method of bringing suppressed matter into consciousness.

The question here is no longer whether one ought to allow everything to come to mind, but whether it is permissible for the patient to bind himself "contractually" to express everything without reservation. Almost everyone has secrets which he may not confide even to his analyst—even at the risk of serious personal disadvantages. In this connection Pius XII said:

> The aspect of psychotherapeutic practice which we just spoke of touches on one of society's vital interests: the obligation to secrecy, which may be endangered by the application of psychotherapy. The possibility is by no means to be excluded that a secret act or item of knowledge may, when forced down into the unconscious, give rise to serious psychic disturbances. When psychoanalysis uncovers the cause of these disturbances it will attempt, in accordance with its fundamental principles, to bring this unconscious material completely into the open in order to remove the obstacle. But there are secrets about which it is absolutely necessary to keep silent, even before a practitioner, and even at the risk of serious personal damage. The secret of the confessional permits of no disclosure. In the same way an official secret may not be imparted, even to a doctor. And this applies also to other secrets. Appeal is made to the principle that it is permissible, for sufficiently grave reasons, to reveal a secret to a discreet and prudent man. This principle is valid within restricted limits for certain types of secret. But it may not be applied without restraint in psychoanalytical practice. Where morality, and especially the common good, is

concerned it is impossible to overemphasize the principle of discretion in the application of psychoanalysis. It is, of course, not the discretion of the psychoanalyst which is primarily at issue here, but that of his patient, who frequently has no right whatever to expose his secrets.

M.: If I understand you rightly you are distinguishing between two types of secrets here; the secrets which everyone has to keep, and so-called official secrets. We come across the latter with patients who are bound to silence about certain matters for professional reasons. But evidently, no violence is done to the psychoanalytical rule if, say, a politician, a doctor or a priest conceals his professional secrets or communicates them in such a way that the analyst cannot possibly be described as a confidant. This can be compared with what happens among priests: if a priest talks with a colleague about things he has actually heard from a penitent he will not be violating the seal of confession so long as he outlines the facts of the case in such a way as to prevent a third party from sharing in the actual secret. Anyone entrusted with objective secrets can act in the same way during analysis. But these cases are borderline situations and comparatively rare.

More typical are the secrets you first spoke of. These form part of everyone's life, and while there is no juridical obligation to keep them, there may certainly be a moral one. But here two different attitudes can be encountered during the analytical treatment of neurotic disturbances. In the first case the patient thinks that he is exposing himself, in the other that he is exposing a third party. These impressions are often justified by an appeal to the moral obligation to secrecy. But such secrets do not form an exception to the fundamental rule of analysis. To an inexperienced outsider this may appear "immoral". In reality, however, a person is required to be unreservedly honest only about himself.

The principle can perhaps be made clearer if we think of the sort of facts which a patient may rate as moral secrets and thus withhold from analysis for a very long time. With one woman patient it was two years before she could bring herself, and only with great pain and difficulty, to speak of a "theft" she had committed as a fifteen-year-old girl. She had found in the street a purse containing fifty Reichsmarks and had not handed it in to the police. She had never been able to speak of this "crime" to anyone, not even her husband. I was the first person to whom she had ever admitted this distressing act, and she was sixty-two when she told me.

Another example: a schizophrenic patient for a long time concealed his hallucinations from the therapist. At a later stage of treatment he accounted for his attitude by saying that his voices belonged to him alone and were his personal property.

Both examples help to illustrate the fundamental principle. The subjective impression that one has secrets to keep is often a cover for attitudes characteristic of the patient's personality and symptoms. Subjectively these patients have just as much right to keep silent as those who refuse to give up their belief in the stars or their conviction that they are immortal. They are all afraid of their belief being destroyed, yet—and this is the decisive element—they are quite unable to say why.

If you release a person from talking about such things by pointing out the moral obligation to secrecy at the very start it will never be possible for him to detach himself from ideas and experiences which may be morbid, immature or even dangerous. This would be simply to set up resistances. And it goes to confirm a tendency closely bound up with the neurotic condition: a perfectly right and proper principle is applied in the interests of the neurosis and then used during treatment as a form of resistance.

Much the same goes for cases where a third party is concerned. I might here mention the woman who never dared to say that her husband snored. She thought this would be exposing him to the analyst.

The fundamental rule of analysis rests on the assumption that the patient has full confidence in the analyst. If the patient should ever get the impression that the therapist is making improper use of the secrets entrusted to him, or is not keeping them to himself, his suspicion must be frankly and thoroughly discussed. In most cases the suspicion turns out to be a central symptom of the neurosis and thus functions as a resistance which makes it impossible for psychotherapy to achieve any successful breakthrough.

E.: You are envisaging secrets which are bound up with the suppressed elements of personal experience. But another aspect of the Pope's objection must be taken into account, and again it concerns those things which come straight to mind and may or may not be expressed without internal resistances during the course of free association. A patient must have the right to stand aside from the terms of the contract and leave unspoken things which are dear to him or which burden other people. I am thinking, for instance, of very intimate religious experiences or really burdensome family secrets.

On principle you will probably allow the patient here to inform the analyst that personal reasons make it impossible for him to express what he is thinking. A psychotherapist will know from the way it is said that this is no unconscious resistance but simply a reticence dictated by a conscious moral decision. But the moment the analyst senses that the refusal is a cover for something to do with the neurosis under treatment he will do his best to bring the patient to speak about it naturally and discreetly. And in this case the patient, too, will have the moral right to confide his secret to the psycho-therapist as far as is necessary, since the cure he desires constitutes a sufficiently grave reason. It remains a borderline case when neither the analyst nor the patient are immediately clear about the best thing to do, but this will simply have to be accepted as inevitable. Difficulties in individual cases are no argument against the basic principle. It is quite clear that the psychotherapist both can and must expect his patient to trust him.

c) The patient's obligation not to discuss treatment with outsiders

M.: There is one more thing to be said on the subject of secrets. We are accustomed to enjoin patients as far as possible not to talk about what has been said or experienced in analysis, except, of course, for superficialities and relatively peripheral things about the analytical process. This rule is designed to help the patient to become independently and personally aware of his own experiences, thoughts, notions and feelings, without mixing them up with other people's views. The patient should not even recount his dreams to others.

This point in particular is very often not understood at first. But the principle will become apparent if it is borne in mind that everyone is naturally inclined to dismiss the products of his inner self as triviality or hot air. People often feel instinctively that their notions, fantasies and dreams have something to do with their own persons, even if they do not know what. They try to take the edge off information which should most certainly be taken seriously by telling it to other people. A dream is much "funnier" and much less important for other people than it is for oneself. If a patient listens to another person's reaction he will be less able to take the matter seriously and form his own opinion, which only makes it all the more difficult for the analysis to go any deeper.

E.: However good and understandable the reasons a psychotherapist may have for requiring his patient not to talk about what has been said during analysis, they cannot be declared absolutely binding from the point of view of moral and pastoral theology. The healing of neurosis is not an ultimate good in itself: for a Christian the most important thing is salvation in accordance with the will of God. Now it may well happen that analysis arouses grave conscientious doubts in the patient. Although in many cases these may be simply neurotic evasions without any objective foundation, there may be other cases where they are genuine, either when the spiritual development of the patient during analysis has resulted in moral and religious distress, or when there has been misconduct on the part of the analyst, who may have been offending against professional ethics by subjecting the patient to ideological influence or attempting to exploit the situation created by analysis for erotic purposes. Neither of these dangers will apply in the case of conscientious and skilled analysts, but, as you yourself have said, there are not enough of them.

It has to be taken into account that someone may set himself up as an analyst and perhaps even have a number of successes to his credit, and yet be, on the whole, inadequately trained and experienced, and, what is most important, without sufficient human qualifications for this profession. It may then happen that, as a result of ignorance or human weakness, the analysis is used as a means of imposing the analyst's own ideas and wishes upon the patient, and in this case the patient must in principle be free to have recourse to a spiritual adviser. I could easily conceive of cases where the analytical process would only benefit from this, especially when the analyst and the spiritual adviser come together for discussion. Admittedly, in a good number of cases the spiritual adviser would have unconditionally to recommend that treatment be broken off. It is, of course, important that advice on such points be sought only from priests who are familiar at least with the basic principles of psychotherapy and are able to recognize when there is reason to suppose that the patient's distress is not a genuinely moral and religious phenomenon but simply a neurotic attempt to break away from analysis. Because it is so important that this "emergency exit" to the priest (or, for that matter, to another specialist or the public prosecutor) should always be left open, it is most unadvisable for a priest with psychotherapeutic training to carry out a (major) therapeutic analysis while acting at the same time as a spiritual adviser. It has rightly been pointed out (Ph. Dessauer) that the patient will turn to him at one moment as analyst, and at the next as priest, which will greatly reduce the chances of success. *M.:* In principle I would agree with you, though I would express the conclusions somewhat differently. If an analyst uses the treatment as a means of living out his own personal problems, whether erotic or ideological, the patient should break off analysis, and if necessary take appropriate legal action. But these primitive abuses, which would have been more likely to occur in the early days of psychoanalysis than they are today, particularly as far as ideological pressure is concerned, are probably no more frequent than the occasional misuse of the confessional by priests. Non-Catholics sometimes imagine the most fantastic things about the confessional.

But possibilities of this sort apart, patients generally have a very keen sense for irregularities which are much less conspicuous; in most cases they will break off treatment without consulting anyone else. They find out fairly quickly whether they are able to place their confidence in an analyst or not, or whether he has the professional and human qualities necessary for his psychotherapeutic work. It must be borne in mind that the analyst has to give his patients the "why's and wherefores" of everything he says and does. We do not work under "narcosis" or—as is occasionally assumed—by means of various gimmicks which reduce the patient's powers of judgment. We offer the patient our experience, our method and our willingness to help. It is then up to him alone to decide whether he wants to make use of us or not.

Exceptions to this rule are people with certain types of mental illness. For a start, they are in no position to grasp what really goes on in psychotherapy. They are afraid of being influenced negatively or injured by words or looks. But these are symptoms which the people affected will have even outside the consulting-room. The therapeutic technique in these cases will be different from that for neuroses, which means that this is a separate question. But we will have occasion later to come back again to the distinctive characteristics of the emotional relationship between analyst and patient.

2. Dangers from newly conscious psychic elements

E.: The moral theologian will direct his questioning and critical gaze not only upon the method by which the various repressions leading to arrested development are brought into the open, but also upon the various aspects of this newly-won consciousness itself.

a) *The purpose of making psychic elements conscious*

E.: Before going into individual questions, or, for that matter, before expressing doubts and criticisms, it is important to be quite clear about the purpose served by causing repressed psychic elements to come gradually to consciousness. After you have given us some information on this point I will come to my critical questions.

M.: The decisive and really efficacious factor in treatment is not theoretical knowledge about some particular aspect of one's personality. If that were the case it would be possible to make therapy a great deal simpler. A good test and a few interviews would be sufficient to establish certain character symptoms and their origins. The patient would then have learned something about himself—though certainly not so profoundly and thoroughly as during the course of psycho-therapy.

Self-knowledge of this sort can produce results, but it does not make it possible to effect any substantial alteration in the dynamics of personality. To start with, every character change which might be effected in this way would be governed excessively by the understanding and the will, and hence would consume a lot of energy, quite apart from the "superficiality" of such "transformations". A priest will be quite familiar with "improvements" of this sort from the confessional. A thorough-going examination of conscience can reveal certain weaknesses and mobilize the understanding and the will to remove them. Not infrequently, however, the penitent is left with the old failings, which he is finally forced to look on as a divinely imposed cross; unless, of course, he spreads a "cloak of virtue" over them, thus making it all the harder to turn over any new leaf. This is not intended as a criticism of examination of conscience or of natural moral effort. But these are inadequate when it comes to symptoms whose roots lie so deep in the personality that they cannot be reached by an examination of conscience.

This also serves to outline another aspect of psychoanalysis as it really is. Its purpose is not to bring the patient to know more about himself but to help him fulfil himself by enabling him to gain a mature command over aspects of his personality which had previously been unknown to him while working themselves out in symptoms. Freud summed up this process as follows: "Where ID was, EGO must come to be." But this is only possible in a dialogue with another person in which a certain degree of self-knowledge helps bring into play things which in earlier phases of life were hidden from the Ego and could not be freely admitted to consciousness.

E.: Depth psychology, by attending to these negative aspects, helps to explain more clearly what ethics and pedagogy can learn from a modern psychology of the will: that will-power does not exist in isolation as something which can be switched on when needed. All activation of the will depends on the object of a voluntary decision taking its subjective value from affective experience, and the dynamism of motivation has to be aroused by means of emotional desires and value-associations before an act of will can be made. None of this is possible if the "depths" of the soul—its inmost ground of being—is unable to work its way into conscious experience. When this process breaks down it means that the affective experiences and normal motivational impulses are being inhibited by some neurosis, and it is very much in the interests of religious and moral life itself that repressions should be made conscious so that the functions of the psyche may be "de-jammed". All the same, there remain some queries and doubts. The first of these is very general in nature and can probably be dealt with quite quickly.

b) Danger of over-consciousness

E.: Is consciousness always such a desirable thing? One does not need by a long chalk to be a disciple of Ludwig Klages to suggest that it is possible to be too conscious of one's vital functions. If a person has a needlessly high degree of control over the activity of his organs he will only interfere with their proper functioning. The effects will probably be even less happy in the psychic sphere if a person is consciously reflecting on his every action, as though he were constantly looking at himself in a mirror. This will make him virtually incapable of any vigorous, unconstrained response to values, whether in thought or in act. Might it be said that psychoanalysis, particularly when successful, results in a psychological self-centredness which deprives a person of all vitality and all ability to devote himself to another person or to some course of action? What appears so disturbing about some people who have undergone analysis is the sense that they know themselves so well as to be past all disillusionment. Might not such perfection of self-awareness block the way to the deeper mysteries of human existence and make a true Christian life impossible? Psychological self-centredness of this sort might very easily make a person egocentric in the moral sense, too, and lead in many cases to a perhaps very highly cultivated egoism. Asceticism can present a similar danger. The struggle for self-perfection, with its painfully precise and technically complete control of conscious actions, can make a person miss the main point of Christ's whole teaching: that a man will find his life by "losing" it, by listening to God's promptings and giving himself to God and his neighbour.

The rule in moral theology is to forget oneself as much as possible and to know oneself as much as need be. It is by far the finer thing to respond unconstrainedly and generously to moral values. But psychotherapy, it would seem, aims at maximum consciousness?

M.: I think this point is very important, and not only for moral reasons. Psychological aspects come into it as well. These are quite often brought up by the patient at the beginning of analytical treatment, and they are sometimes responsible for treatment not being taken up in the first place, however badly it may be needed. It can happen, for example, that mothers, advised to undergo psychotherapeutic treatment because of their children's developmental difficulties, are afraid that this might make it impossible for them to bring up their children according to their "natural maternal instincts" and that they might lose their confidence if they underwent therapy. They, too, believe that analytic treatment leads to over-consciousness, and that constant introspection will make them unable to live their lives out properly. It is characteristic that this fear is expressed mainly at the beginning of analysis, and more often still before the decision to undergo it has been taken. But once they have actually "taken the plunge" their fears increasingly evaporate. It might be said, then, that the more seriously a patient takes his analysis and the more frank and open he is the more able he becomes to live freely and without constraint. At all events, he will not be constantly reflecting upon things which have been worked through during analysis. We even advise a patient occasionally not to think consciously about what has been accomplished. On the whole, in fact, we tend to be even more sceptical about all types of reflections and deliberate intentions than the pastoral theologian.

How is this to be explained? Individual differences aside, the answer can perhaps be usefully summarized in terms of your "ascetical" principle: to forget oneself as much as possible and to know oneself as much as need be. Psychotherapeutic treatment increases a person's degree of self-knowledge as far as is necessary to help him master his life in self-forgetfulness. Without this knowledge a person is much more likely to keep stumbling over his neurotic character, his heart complaints, the fancied lovelessness of his wife or the overwhelming burden of his work. Or would you say, for instance, that the manager who thoughtlessly sacrifices his family life to business and politics is a self-forgetful man given to values? In the case of a man like this the fear of over-consciousness may seem, at least, to be a credible motive for refusing psychotherapy; but with some hypochondriacs it will strike even the layman as a subterfuge. They utterly fail to notice that their anxiety about physical ills, their heart or their lungs, is simply a "pathological introversion", and so they think they can refuse psycho-therapeutic treatment with a "good conscience", making use, in fact, of the reasons you have brought forward.

Incidentally, there is scarcely any difference, psycho-dynamically speaking, between hypochondriacs and people who experience their over-consciousness as a psychic symptom and for that very reason come for psychotherapeutic treatment. They cannot do anything, or talk or read or think, without constantly watching themselves. As a result, quite ordinary little tasks demand a major effort of will. People in this position often sense that something must be amiss. But if there were ground for your fears treatment could only make their condition worse. But the very opposite is the case. They are liberated from their introspection and are enabled to respond more spontaneously and meaningfully to the world around them.

c) Modes in which repressed matter comes to be experienced

E.: A little while back we were talking about Pius XII's objections to the practice of free association. We shall have to refer to this again because the Pope's real concern was perhaps not brought out fully and precisely enough. The question is no longer the desirability of allowing everything to come to mind, but rather the actual way in which a patient experiences the concepts through which hitherto repressed matter is brought to consciousness.

The moral theologian would have no misgivings if the patient simply reported in a matter-of-fact way that such and such thoughts were passing through his mind. In reality, however, the repressed psychic content now entering the consciousness is often charged with emotions and instinctive impulses. To illustrate this I will give the example of a young girl who up to now has made great sacrifices to care for her constantly ailing and extremely demanding mother, and who has considered this filial love as a form of necessary moral trial; yet during analysis she is suddenly aware that burning feelings of hate for her mother are breaking through. This is no longer a cool, matter-of-fact account but an emotional experience very near the level of responsible consciousness; in accordance with her whole ethical attitude the girl must reject it as morally undesirable. May the young lady give way to these feelings or must she turn her mind against them at once? This example may help to make clear why Pius XII found the activation of such emotions very questionable.

M.: To set this moral problem in somewhat more concrete terms I should like, if I may, to give the following rather simplified example. A man comes to the consulting-room, suffering from acute impotence. He has been married three or four years without being able to consummate his marriage. Consultation with various specialists and all sorts of treatment have brought no improvement. Finally a doctor has referred him to a psychotherapist. Now it may happen during treatment that the patient has a dream in which his penis appears insignificantly small and totally useless. During the course of free association he may perhaps recall that his parents paid a negative and unnatural attention to his member. As a child he was expected to restrict all washing to the necessary minimum and was severely punished if he indulged in playful handling out of curiosity or pleasure. In short, the family was pervaded by an atmosphere which subdued all the joy the possession of this organ will have at a certain age, and turned it into a source of uneasiness and finally of contempt.

Analysis, then, can give rise to situations where the therapist encourages the patient to think about his anatomically intact member more positively and pleasurably than he has hitherto permitted himself.

Now, would the moral theologian say that the analyst must stop here, or at least see that his patient turns his mind as quickly as possible to a "morally permissible" theme? Or are you of the opinion that the patient may be urged on to such thoughts?

E.: A moral theologian would take a positive attitude here. It is an important aspect of moral self-realization to accept ourselves as God has created us and to do so in the way intended by him. Sexuality is obviously included, and sexuality cannot be experienced without the corresponding feelings and instincts. If a person's past life has atrophied this experience, encouragement must be given to any method which puts any mutilations and distortions right. There is a factor here which we have already touched upon and which the moral theologian terms the *actio cum duplici effectu*: man intends something good in itself for a good end. There are situations where man cannot attain the good without cheerfully accepting what might be morally dangerous. If this is the case and the good is predominant then it is permissible to expose oneself even to something which is potentially dangerous. The moral theologian, too, must wish that man and wife should really become fully aware of one another and experience their physical sexuality. This is an absolutely necessary condition if the moral personality is to mature. If temptations arise in the process they will simply have to be faced.

But the example you have chosen does not focus the moral problem sharply enough, since the experience here is a morally unexceptionable one, given the right setting and the right intention. How, though, is one to judge the experience during analysis of psychic matter which is quite obviously morally objectionable, such as the hatred felt by the girl towards her mother? I should like to try and clarify this difficult question, because the moral theologians themselves are not unanimous.

First of all, it must be stated that it can never be morally permissible to consent, freely and deliberately, to rising feelings of hatred, as, for example, when in everyday life one comes up against an unpleasant and malicious competitor. All moral theologians are agreed here. In the same way, then, a patient under analysis may give a matter-of-fact report of these emotional uprisings, but not identify himself with them in any way; he must reject them immediately.

M.: A psychoanalyst would have to register a protest here, because what you are suggesting would completely obstruct one of the indispensable conditions of psychic healing. If repressed elements are to be made fully conscious and worked through thoroughly they will first have to be affirmed; otherwise the resistances which led to the repression will never be removed.

Psychologically speaking, your viewpoint is justified only where the repressed impulses have not worked themselves out in symptoms—in other words, where the repression has been successful. But this is not so with the people to whom we have been referring.

E.: All the same, a number of serious and authoritative moral theologians say that the repression will have to stay as it is, since no end can ever justify a morally objectionable means, and to affirm or give free rein to feelings of hatred is morally objectionable in itself.

On the other hand, a more cautious and sensitive argument has been put forward by A. Snoeck, S.J., which I myself would describe as a probable opinion. During analysis we are no longer confronted with a normal condition of human personality but with something more like a psychic fever in which the healing process takes place; this is particularly true of transference, since this involves a very special link between patient and therapist which will have to be discussed later. The patient's state is one of dissociation, a disruption of spiritual experience; this was already present in repressed form, but is now being brought into the open by analysis. The question is, where are these feelings of hatred coming from? Not from the core of the patient's personality, but, so to speak, from the child the patient once was; analysis has to make the patient become this child again, so that he can retrace his developmental disturbances and approach them in a more healthy state of mind. In this situation the patient is not fully in control of himself, however vividly he may experience the feelings of hatred. The child he once was now forces itself into his consciousness: the repressions, which will usually have taken place in early childhood, caused his impressions during the stage of development preceding the age of reason to be deep-frozen and overlaid. A breath of air stirs these impressions back into life, and the consequent reaction could be described by the moral theologian as an *actus hominis* as opposed to an *actus humanus*—in other words, an event which, though conscious, is not psychologically under full control. The previously repressed matter has been brought by analysis to a transitional stage, which is a sort of "fever", and constitutes a quasi-autonomous "secondary centre" of the psyche, thus taking such hold of the patient when he becomes conscious of it that he is deprived of his full freedom of decision and hence of full moral responsibility. The patient will be caught up more or less by the feelings of hatred so long as he persists in his intention of "persevering with analysis"; unless, of course, he forcefully tears himself away from the experience and dissociates himself from it, which would disturb the healing process, if not destroy it altogether. As analysis progresses the patient will, of course, have to get to work on what has been recalled to consciousness and try, so to speak, to become himself once more in the new situation.

d) The hazard to psychic equilibrium

E.: We have already referred occasionally to one specific danger of making psychic content conscious or increasing a patient's self-awareness. But might one not conceive of borderline cases where the activation of repressed drives or elements of consciousness unleashes an "emotional storm" with which the person affected is not yet capable of coping? This need not necessarily be in the sexual sphere, simply the shock felt at confronting a reality about oneself which has previously remained unknown. I am thinking of a case in the specialist literature of a brother and sister who were emotionally very much attached to one another. After the marriage of one of them had broken down they both underwent psychoanalysis. It turned out that their relationship went beyond that of brother and sister and was basically erotic in nature. So great was their shock that they committed suicide.

M.: I do not know the case myself, but the problem you have raised was set out during the 'twenties by Alfred Seidel in his book *Das Bewusstsein als Verhängnis*. The author committed suicide, and, to judge from his papers, for the very reason you have in mind: the confrontation with the unconscious. It was often used as an objection to psychoanalysis and to some extent still is—as your own allusion shows.

If the assumption that a confrontation with the unconscious constitutes a danger to life is correct, then suicides during analytical treatment could hardly fail to occur more frequently. There would necessarily be a high "mortality rate" in much the same way as with serious surgical operations. But this is not the case. On the contrary—very many people with suicidal intentions are liberated from their impulse by psychoanalysis.

E.: Perhaps I could put the question in more general terms. Are there not cases where analysis might bring to consciousness things which the patient is as yet incapable of coping with and which plunge him into spiritual chaos? If the psychotherapist recognizes such a danger is it permissible for him to continue with analysis, or should he intervene and even, if necessary, break off analysis?

M.: If the psychotherapist recognizes a serious and immediate danger to the patient or his environment he will most certainly intervene. But cases like this are probably rare. More important is the fact that there are often transitional phases during psychoanalytical treatment which the patient finds threatening. These appear frequently as clinical symptoms, such as anxiety or depression. The therapist must find out what significance these have before he can get to work on them the right way. Such phases can be compared with certain developmental crises. These crisis symptoms mark a reshuffling of psychic elements, and there is a tendency to shrink back from the task of coming to grips with the new situation. Moral problems can also play a part here.

The main outlines can be illustrated with the aid of an example. A woman aged forty-four, married and with two children, lives in the same town as her seventy-year-old mother. Previously they lived in the same house together, but this led to constant friction between the mother and her daughter and son-in-law and finally to her departure. But from her new abode the mother will not stop interfering in her daughter's marriage and family life and constantly keeps up contact by means of telephone calls or unexpected visits. She is either requiring medicines or asking for shopping to be done or expecting her daughter to come and look after her. The daughter, believing as she does in the commandment to love one's parents, complies with these wishes, quite unaware that her mother's behaviour is unreasonable and demanding. Scenes with her husband become more and more frequent, but she does not connect them in any way with her attitude towards her mother. In this situation she decides to go for psychoanalytical therapy, and in the course of treatment her attitude towards her mother undergoes a transformation: the apparently obedient and self-sacrificing daughter begins to revolt against her mother's demands. She becomes rebellious and is no longer prepared to obey. The mother reacts with choking-fits and allusions to imminent death, thus plunging the daughter into a conflict between "filial love" and legitimate self-fulfilment.

The problem I want to outline briefly here can be put as follows. During psychoanalysis it is possible for attitudes to undergo changes whose most critical effects are felt by people in the patient's immediate environment, and most particularly by the parents. If the patient has not succeeded in breaking away from his parents in the normal and desirable way, with all the consequences of this failure as regards mature integration, then serious conflicts can arise in later years. Characteristically, they are not always seen as conflicts with the parents, but much more frequently as difficulties in marriage, or with the children, or at work. If, then, analysis brings to consciousness certain immature attitudes towards parents which have survived since childhood, the patient will often undergo a moral crisis. He will mostly feel his inclinations to be an offence against filial love rather than a necessary obligation to self-fulfilment.

So long as I state the problem in these terms even the moral theologian will not hesitate to emphasize the moral obligation to individual integrity and fulfilment, even if it means accepting temporary crises for the patients and certain ill-feelings on the part of the parents. But the pattern of events very rarely strikes the outsider as clearly as in this example. Unassailable arguments are usually put forward—my parents are old, ill, or lonely, they may soon die. And so it is perfectly understandable for patients with such problems to turn repeatedly for advice to a friend or confessor who simply considers this compliance with parental demands as a moral duty. But when the grown-up child attempts to make his own demands felt—which often enough is possible only under analysis—his rebellion against his parents may temporarily build up to feelings of deep hatred. Outsiders are then quite often indignant and say that treatment has turned obedient children into wicked rebels.

E.: On principle a moral theologian would also emphasize the obligation to self-fulfilment, even where this may upset the relationship with the parents. What the children are becoming conscious of here is probably not real hatred at all but simply a legitimate indignation at the years during which their liberty has been restricted. After all—as in your example— the woman is there in the first place for her husband and children, and for this reason, too, she is obliged to make herself inwardly free for this task. And I think we would even go a step further. The problem has been fundamentally reversed: in her unfortunate situation the mother herself is now the child, and the daughter, while remaining firm, should have pity on her.

M.: But it was precisely this pity and sympathy which led to long-suffering acceptance of parental demands in the first place. Many parents even arrange pitiable symptoms so that the children may remain dependent on them even long after they have grown up. Unconscious arrangement should not, though, be imagined as a sort of deliberate "staging", as the layman occasionally assumes, but as a "conditioned reflex". It is rather like what happened in Pavlov's famous experiment, where an association was set up between a ringing bell and the secretion of gastric juices—over the years an association comes to be formed between independent behaviour on the part of the children and symptoms of illness on the part of the mother or the father. This functions quite "automatically" and is frequently a much more effective means of imposing one's will than severe punishment. Because of the child's natural willingness and his moral obligation to compassion, suffering can do more violence than the rod.

While moral theologians will not consider such abuses as legitimate in principle, they do tend to base their judgments on external aspects; as a result they become unable to discriminate between use and abuse.

E.: Your warning to priests should be taken seriously. When I spoke of pity and of the reversal of the child–parent relationship I was really envisaging cases where daughters or sons have already shaken off their bondage and completely resisted parental demands, so that at last they can start to devote themselves properly to their families or their work. Although, in cases like these, one may have come to realize the necessity of taking a firm stand, one may not always find it all that easy; and it can help to bolster self-confidence and make it easier to be kind but firm if one remembers that the parents, because of their dependence, are no longer figures to be held in filial awe but are themselves starting to be "children"—or perhaps always have been.

For the rest, I will admit that many of us priests do allow ourselves to be taken in by too much generalization when judging the behaviour of individuals. We tend to assume that if the externals of an act are moral then the act itself will be moral too. But this is simply a danger which must be kept clearly in mind and thus avoided as far as possible.

e) Activation of urges beyond all power of control

E.: From the moral theologian's point of view there is another possible effect of newly-found consciousness which is more important than temporary confusion, anxiety or depression. If repressed and pent-up urges are brought to consciousness, might they not express themselves so violently that it becomes simply impossible to keep them under moral control? I am thinking, say, of a very "piously" educated young man who, under analysis, becomes conscious of his previously repressed inclination towards the female sex, and is then swept off his feet by a sudden turmoil of sexual desires, thus becoming—for the time being, at least—sexually demoralized. An expert psychotherapist will, of course, do his best to prepare the patient for possibly dangerous pieces of self-knowledge in such a way that any undesirable developments can be forestalled. *M.:* This, in fact, is just what the competent psychotherapist will always be doing. Ultimately, psychoanalysis overcomes the inclination to remain fixed at an earlier stage of development by using the dialogue with the analyst and the emotional processes involved in order to show the patient the advantages of mature relationships. To put it in a slightly different way: the relationship with the therapist makes viable certain aspects of the personality which, because of earlier experiences, have been cut off from normal development. It is just as though a new leg were growing to replace one which had been amputated, so that the person can now go through life with both legs. This process of growth may involve temporary crises, possibly even externally immoral behaviour. But, as you have said, these phases must simply be put up with if the patient is to attain to full personal maturity and lead a moral life based on genuine conviction.

f) Ethically impermissible consequences of treatment

E.: But more important and more difficult than these cases—which will probably be fairly rare anyway—is the question as to how the therapist should behave when he recognizes during analysis the first signs, and even the first stirrings, of developments which for ethical reasons should not go any further. May the analyst approve, and even go so far as to recommend, morally impermissible forms of behaviour which result from making repressed matter conscious and use these as a means to the good end of psychic healing?

Let us take an example. A married man, whose marriage has entered a crisis, visits a psychotherapist. In the course of treatment it becomes clear to him that he has married his wife simply because she was a mother-figure and that he feels no personal attachment to her whatsoever. Even sexually she has no appeal for him, and he feels strongly attracted to another woman. The analyst predicts with a high degree of probability that this conflict will lead to adultery. In such a case, can he accept this development and let it go on?

M.: May I answer your question by referring to a case from practice?

A theological student, at a fairly advanced stage of his studies, tried very hard to get permission to undergo psycho-analytical treatment. At first his superiors would not agree. They saw no real reason. This candidate for the priesthood seemed to be a well-balanced personality with a robust faith. Finally he got permission, on the condition, however, that he would work later in the borderline field between moral theology and psychotherapy. His analysis was to be part of his training. I began treatment on the usual terms. During the second session he recounted a dream. Apart from a small question of detail I adopted a passive attitude. At the next session there followed another dream, and during free associa-tion he mentioned, among other things, that my one and only question at the preceding session had given him the impression that I had doubts about his vocation. I told him that the doubt was certainly there, but that after so short an acquaintance it could hardly be sufficiently well-founded for any conclusions to be drawn from it. The patient was relieved by my frankness but thought he should put my mind at rest. He had, he said, no doubts whatever about his vocation, he felt, in fact, more confident about his priesthood than ever before. After a few more sessions he was afflicted by a depression such as he had never known before, and by strong doubts about his faith.

After four more sessions he phoned me before the next appointment and told me he had decided to give up his theological studies, but did not want to come to the next session before he had spoken with his superiors. The superiors would trace the decision to the analyst's influence and try to make him change his mind and continue with his studies. Today the candidate is the head of a happy family in a different walk of life.

Now, what can this case demonstrate in regard to your question?

1. During the course of character development a person may be steered towards a decision of which he is really very little aware. There are several possible reasons for this lack of awareness. It is often connected with the fact that, without realizing it, he is looking at himself or his situation, with all his various obligations, habits and prospects, from a very narrow angle. This angle is often determined exclusively by other people's opinions, but in particular by the opinion of some person he looks up to and to whose judgment he attaches great importance. So long as he remains fixed in this condition he will lack the self-reliance necessary for forming a free decision. For this reason not a few people are saddled with the consequences of mistaken decisions—or semi-decisions— their whole life long. The theology student might perhaps have become a priest, with all the uncertainties and dangers of a "half"-existence.

2. Under certain circumstances the crisis going on in the background of experience can be grasped more clearly by the psychoanalyst than by the person concerned. But the analyst cannot make forecasts with hundred-per-cent accuracy, for the simple reason that he cannot know what line the patient will strike out on when he has become aware of the previously hidden aspects of himself. Once the theology student had confronted the underlying hostilities to his vocation it would

have been "theoretically" possible for him to come to terms with them and thus arrive at a mature decision to continue.

And the same will necessarily apply to your model example. It is not unusual for a married man under analysis to realize that he has married for immature reasons of which he was unaware. The conclusions to be drawn from this vary from case to case. There are far too many factors to be taken into consideration, and the partners and their external circumstances are only two of them. But there is one requirement, and one requirement only, implicit in every analysis—that all decisions should lead, as far as possible, to greater maturity and harmonization. This, after all, is the ultimate aim of analysis. But it is not to be attained through the gratification of immaturities from the distant past. In the case you brought forward this might have been, perhaps, an "ill-considered" marriage with a woman after nothing more than a fleeting acquaintance. To this extent adultery would be neither a necessary nor a desirable consequence.

But in the course of psychoanalytical work we most certainly come across cases where our attitude towards adultery in practice differs considerably from that of the moral theologian. For the moral theologian adultery is always reprehensible, it is always a sin. For the psychotherapist, however, it may represent something essentially positive in individual cases—a step in the direction of human maturity. To my mind, the differences of judgment here probably arise from the method rather than from the matter. The moral theologian is confronted merely with the act and possibly with the conscious motivation. He will know neither the life histories nor the concrete situations of a particular marriage, and most certainly nothing about the deep underlying determinants. For him, every validly contracted marriage is a marriage, and all marriages are equally holy. Adultery is judged and even condemned purely for the fact of its having taken place. But under the analyst's microscope many marriages may well reveal themselves to be mock marriages, and for this reason they may well afford a pretext for evading more fundamental decisions of greater importance for personal existence. Thus we recognize such a thing as a mature adultery which may be affirmed for moral (and not just medical) reasons.

E.: To start with, I should really take you up on your idea of mock marriages, since a moral theologian is unable to accept it as it stands. There is certainly a problem here, but we shall no doubt have a chance to come back to it in a different context. For the moment, we are concerned only with the general principles of psychotherapeutic method. Differences of opinion have been raised here and we must try to clarify them. They will have to be looked at more closely so that we can grasp them properly.

In your opinion, the moral theologian considers only isolated acts and their conscious motives and therefore always condemns adultery, while the psychotherapist knows the situation and the concrete circumstances more intimately and will therefore see adultery in some instances as a step towards greater human maturity. But it seems to me that this does not bring out the difference between our views. The moral theologian, too, is at pains to understand moral life as an integral whole and not just as the sum of isolated acts. He, too, will seek to judge the isolated act mainly from its motives and then from personal history and character development. To show this I will bring forward the age-old concept of the *volitum in causa,* according to which an action may be objectively blameworthy in virtue of earlier decisions made by the person concerned. Take the example of a doctor who has made a serious professional mistake and thus incurred responsibility for the death of a patient. At the critical moment his intentions may have been of the best. But if he had, in fact, at some earlier point realized that there was a serious gap in his medical knowledge, but had begun and continued his practice all the same, then from that moment onwards he was guilty of acquiescing in the future possibility of some professional blunder which might well result from it.

And the moral theologian is also familiar with the concept of the *felix culpa,* which means a transgression whose consequences, by God's gracious disposition, work out ultimately as a blessing. In this sense, anyway, he is not blind to the possibility that an act of adultery *in concreto* might actually be a step towards greater human maturity.

The decisive reason for our differences here seems to me to lie in the fact that the moral theologian acknowledges the aim of psychotherapy—i.e., greater human maturity through psychic healing—as something admittedly very important, but not as an ultimately decisive, absolute norm of human behaviour. Psychic health and the psychological factor of free, mature decision are values of human existence. But these are subordinate to moral and religious values, which are distinguished by the unique inexorability of the demands they make. The Church, therefore, will never be able to countenance the use of anything morally reprehensible as a means to achieving the excellent, and even noble, purpose of psychic healing. Personal salvation is more important than psychic healing.

M.: You are here imputing to us a concept of psychic health which is theoretically foreign to psychoanalysis. In all its ideas of health and maturity psychoanalysis always includes moral maturity. To be sure, we differ in what we accept as the criteria of this maturity. For the analyst the distinctive criterion would probably be the capacity for personal love, while the moral theologian, for reasons of method, will pay less attention to such internal attitudes. But we shall have to go further into this later.

E.: When someone is doing something which objectively is

morally impermissible, but is doing it in good faith—in other words, without being aware of the moral reprehensibility of his behaviour—the priest will often keep silent and allow the thing to go on; he does this if he foresees that his intervention might turn a material sin into a formal sin, or, to put it less technically, if the person concerned might simply defy the warning and continue his action from then onwards as a deliberate sin. But something objectively sinful, such as adultery, may never be affirmed; nor, even, may it be recommended as something merely materially sinful. There can be no mistaking the meaning of Pius XII's words: "One last thing must be emphasized about the transcendental nature of the psyche as something directed towards God. Reverence for God and his holiness should always be reflected in the conscious commissions and omissions of man. When man's behaviour—even without any subjective guilt on the part of the doer—diverges from the divine model it contradicts its ultimate purpose. This is the reason why even so-called 'material sin' is something which ought not to be, and why it is not a matter of indifference in the moral order. There is a conclusion to be drawn from this by psychotherapists. They may not be indifferent to material sin. They may tolerate what, for the moment, is unavoidable. But they must realize that God cannot approve of this behaviour. Even less may psychotherapists advise patients to continue unhesitatingly doing something materially wrong because it would be without any subjective guilt. This advice is misguided even when such behaviour might seem necessary for the release of the patient's psychic tensions, and thus advantageous to the healing process. No one may ever recommend any conscious behaviour which is a distortion, and not an image, of divine perfection."

M.: A doctor will generally never allow himself to form a judgment as to whether God approves of the patient's

D

behaviour or not. However deep his faith this is something he cannot do. And as to God's views about concrete cases, I doubt whether a theologian can ever enjoy the accurate knowledge which seems to be implied by the Pope's suggestion that "God cannot approve of this behaviour".

Generally the psychoanalyst does not give advice, particularly in such personal matters as adultery. We do, however, try to analyse behaviour as comprehensively as possible, so that the patient may be enabled to recognize his unconscious motivations more clearly. The intention here is that he should know what he is deciding for and what he is deciding against. Ultimately the decision will always be his own, together with the consequences which flow from it.

Anyone who thinks we would actively or passively approve of an action simply because it effected a temporary release has a mistaken idea about psychoanalysis. Freud himself pointed to the principle that psychoanalytical treatment should be carried out under the "bell-glass of denial", a notion which probably runs clean counter to the ideas many laymen have about the nature of psychoanalysis. People often think that the more possibilities a patient has for releasing his tensions the better it will be for the purpose of treatment. This is not so. One need only think of the various addictions, such as morphinism. Psychotherapeutic treatment is, to all intents and purposes, impossible while the craving is present. Exceptions only go to confirm the rule. The addiction must first be broken by medical means. With a number of less dramatic addictions we have what might be described as our own set of commandments designed to ward off the danger of demoralization. Thus a certain frustration of impulses is always necessary.

I have another question here about the passivity of the analyst.

Let us assume that the theology student we spoke of earlier had already been ordained. Supposing I had gained the impression that his faith was definitely arid and sterile, nothing more, in fact, than an ideology; and that there was clearly a danger of his abandoning his vocation.

Given this danger, what is the moral theologian's view of the procedure to be observed in analysis?

E.: I should say that one must again look more closely. The analyst might, perhaps, form the conviction that there was never any free, rational decision as regards ordination and that the sacrament had therefore not been validly received. It could then be only to the good that he should continue with the analysis, since it is important that the patient should come to terms with something he has been more or less deliberately shirking.

Presumably it is not this you have in mind so much as the by no means unusual case where a candidate, under the influence of environment, parents and teachers, has allowed himself to be steered into the priesthood; his step to the altar was made in all sincerity, though with not very much "existential" awareness. The lack of personal depth in this decision then leads to the neurotic symptoms for which he is consulting the psychotherapist.

I would here make a distinction. If it appears that the course of analysis will bring on a crisis and it is gradually realized that the earlier resolve will have to be integrated into a genuinely radical decision based on deep personal conviction, and if, to the best of human knowledge, there is a good chance of success, then I would go on with the analysis. Any danger of the crisis ending badly should be tolerated for the sake of the important object to be achieved.

But things would be different if, from a knowledge of the patient's personality and from the course of analysis, the analyst should become convinced that such a crisis would cause the patient's vocation to collapse. If there is reason for supposing that, if a crisis is not brought on, the priest will continue sincerely and steadily in his vocation, even at the cost of the symptoms remaining, the factors which might lead up to a crisis should not, in my opinion, be brought to consciousness.

M.: All the same, it should not be forgotten that with these "half-believing priests", it is a matter not only of their own personal fate but also of the people entrusted to their care. I do not think it is honest simply to "stick it out". We shall be talking later about the credibility of witnesses, and further details can be discussed then.

E.: I should like to try and summarize all this in more general terms. When it is a question of whether or not to allow a patient to learn things about himself which probably can or even will set off a morally reprehensible development, then the procedure will have to follow the principle we have already referred to: that it is permissible to aim at a morally good objective even when this unavoidably involves evil consequences, the gravity and likelihood of which have been weighed up against the object to be achieved—in this case the process of healing. It must not be forgotten that no-one can be brought to moral responsibility without at the same time being exposed to temptations which enable him to exercise his power of judgment in the first place. If, in spite of every precaution on the part of the psychotherapist, the newly-found consciousness of certain experiences has led the patient to behave in a way which objectively will end in moral catastrophe, then it will generally have to be assumed that subjectively he was not fully responsible, or that he has used his newly-found freedom irresponsibly, as is, of course, the case with any sin. The blame should most certainly not be laid at the door of the psychoanalyst so long as he has done all in his power to help his patient attain maturity without exposing him to psychic and, especially, moral burdens which could have been avoided.

On the other hand, the duty of the psychotherapist to take every precaution will mean that he should, as far as possible, leave a neurotic symptom where it is, at least for the time being, or divert attention from bringing its cause to consciousness, if he foresees that awareness of this cause would only make things worse. It may be better for a person to live his life under the burden of a neurotic symptom, or—in Christian terms—to carry this cross, than to be shattered altogether by newly-conscious insights and obligations which create too many difficulties for him in his particular concrete circumstances. It would be better for the priest to go on bearing certain neurotic burdens than to realize that his decision was the result, say, of an extreme attachment to his mother and thus abandon a priestly vocation which, in spite of his troubles, he is exercising conscientiously. And the same applies when awareness of the causes of a neurosis will wreck a marriage once the person concerned has come to realize that he married his wife, not for her own person, but as a projection of his father or mother image.

The psychologist is tempted to say that the ordination has never formed the object of a proper decision or that no real marriage has ever been contracted, and that the best thing to do is draw the inevitable conclusions. The moral theologian will accept all this when the psychic burdens have been so great that it is hardly possible any longer to speak of a morally responsible decision as regards the ordination or the marriage. In reality, however, one will much more often come across cases where the situation is by no means so extremely clear-cut. To be valid, a marriage does not have to correspond fully to the ideal of marriage, nor even to suggest that it is likely to do so; it need only fulfil the minimal requirements for the sacrament to become effective. If, therefore, the person concerned has joined himself in marriage as the result of a clearly conscious decision to enter into a full community of life, with all the obligations attached thereto, then the marriage is valid both in canon law and in moral theology. Such a marriage may, to a certain extent, constitute a tragedy, or—again in Christian terms—a heavy cross; but it must be persevered in, because tragedy cannot be evaded by sin. And sin there will be if the person concerned is able, as we have assumed, to fulfil his various marital duties, including a sincere good-will towards his partner (even without emotional satisfaction), although his relationship within marriage has not offered him any possibility of personal fulfilment and all the happiness this can bring. In such cases a responsible psychotherapist would, in the theologian's view, have to leave the oppressive neurotic symptom alone for the time being, and perhaps even break off treatment. He will remember that his aim of bringing about the full integrity of psychic functions will not permit him to infringe the higher sphere of moral and religious values to which his patient holds in conscience. Even without the happiness which one could wish for the man and wife and which would have great positive significance for their marriage, they can still live together companionably, showing kindness and doing good to one another and their children.

The psychotherapist must not use a personal moral sin—and it would be a sin to break up a valid marriage, however far from ideal—simply as a means to the end of psychic healing, and one very good reason for this is that it will no longer be in his power to liberate anyone from a sin after it has been committed. Here—one last time—is what Pius XII has said:

> Another part of the transcendental relationship of the psyche is the consciousness of guilt, the consciousness of having offended against a higher law despite recognition of one's obligations. A consciousness which can become a torment and even a grave psychic disturbance.

Psychotherapy is here confronted with a phenomenon which, since it is either predominantly or at least partly of a religious nature, does not belong exclusively to its sphere of competence. No one will deny that there both can be, and not infrequently is, such a thing as an unfounded and morbid sense of guilt. But there may also be a consciousness of real guilt which has not been expiated. Neither psychology nor ethics has an infallible criterion for individual cases, since what goes on in the human conscience when guilt is incurred is too personal and sensitive a process. The important thing, however, is that when a person becomes conscious of genuine guilt he can be healed by no merely psychological treatment. And even if the psychotherapist denies this guilt, perhaps in the best of faith, it still persists. And while the feeling of guilt may be caused to fade away by means of the doctor's authority, or through suggestion and auto-suggestion, the guilt itself remains, and it would be to deceive both themselves and others if psychotherapists tried to remove the consciousness of guilt by asserting that the guilt is no longer there.

The way towards removing guilt lies outside the purely psychological; it lies, as the Christian knows, in repentance and in the sacramental absolution spoken by the priest.

3. Dangers inherent in transference

E.: Up to now my questions have been concerned with a central function of analysis—the bringing to consciousness of repressed matter. But there is another factor in the psychotherapeutic process which is of interest to the moral theologian, and this is the special relationship the patient enters into with the analyst—the so-called transference. In other medical disciplines the patient–doctor relationship would seem to be less close and, especially, not so essential for the healing process. It is much easier to consider an operation, an X-ray or an injection objectively; these are all less dependent than the psychoanalytical method on the doctor's personal attitude towards the patient. The surgeon can perform a good and successful operation even on a patient he does not like, and a specialist for internal diseases can treat a woman patient with whom he has fallen in love. But nothing like this is possible for the psychoanalyst. Psychoanalytical technique at this point cannot be adequately grasped in terms of external rules. Personal attitude forms an essential part of therapy.

This intensive co-operation, moreover, means that the psychotherapist has demands made on him to an extent rare in medical work. We priests, too, are concerned with the individual human soul; yet we will have to admit that our work in the confessional is relatively simply when compared with the constant effort and concentration required of the analyst. We very seldom realize the strain involved in spending two hundred hours and more with one and the same person, hearing about the tiny minutiae of his everyday life, his dreams, fantasies and hidden attitudes, and seeing progress being made so very slowly. And another difficulty is that the analyst has to maintain a benevolent equanimity and detachment towards all the intimate things which are confided to him or even, in many cases, directed against him. No matter whether his patients revere him or mistrust him, declare their love or give vent to animosity—if he is carrying out his analysis as professional ethics require, he will have to take all these utterances calmly and direct them towards their proper and anthropologically meaningful objects.

This, of course, will often be too much for human strength,

at least in comparison with what the confessor has to put up with, and I should like to make this point before coming out more explictly with my own ethical misgivings. These misgivings arise precisely from the close co-operation of two human beings. What I should like to ask first is this: is it morally permissible for the psychotherapist to allow the relationship to become so close that he actually assumes—even if only temporarily—the place of a father or mother or some equally significant figure in the life of his patient?

a) The function of transference in analysis

M.: The only way to show exactly what part this relationship plays in analytical treatment is to bring out clearly how it differs from comparable doctor-patient relationships. A useful example here would be the family doctor of former days, whose disappearance has been deplored both by patients and by quite a large body of opinion in the medical profession. The role he played in family life went far beyond the purely medical, and he was often a sort of personal adviser. The essential difference between this relationship and the type encountered in psychoanalysis can be set out much as follows.

In the case of the family doctor, and in similar relationships such as that of penitent to confessor, people will reflect only to a certain extent on the underlying factors. Generally this will go no further than the simple fact that one happens to like, revere or even love a particular doctor or priest for certain qualities he may possess, and all shades of sympathy are possible. But there is no cause to investigate all the little aspects of temperament and disposition behind such relationships, nor to ask why one person should hold a particular doctor in high esteem while another will have nothing to do with him.

In the case of psychoanalysis, however, all this simply has to be investigated. It is important that the factors underlying the whole multiplicity of inter-human relationships—including that with the psychotherapist—should be closely observed and examined.

The need for such an approach to the matter was discovered by Freud. At a time when most of his colleagues were working with hypnosis he had the experience of a patient awaking from her hypnotic trance and, filled with feelings of love, throwing her arms around him. The experience was probably not an uncommon one at the time, though Freud's reaction may well have been not quite so usual. Unlike a good number of others he was level-headed enough to inquire into the reasons for such behaviour rather than conclude that he must be irresistible. This level-headed inquiry marked the birth of psychoanalysis, and it constituted an entirely new approach to apparently unmotivated transports of emotion.

The emotional interplay between analyst and patient was to become the central and crucial symptom of analytical treatment. It does, in fact, offer the best means of detecting the difficulties in ordinary life and making them accessible to the patient's consciousness. The symptoms of almost all psychic disturbances are always at least partly disturbances in human relationships, and they will have been acquired from the human beings with whom the patient was first confronted and from whom he formed his first impressions. It is the aim of psychoanalysis to reach back to the experiences of this stage of life, and in order to do this the analyst adopts a predominantly passive attitude—in contrast, again, to the patient's other human relationships. The intention behind this is to create a situation in which the earliest modalities of confrontation may be consciously re-lived and made as clear and intelligible as possible.

Psychoanalysis is only secondarily a process of interpretation.

Primarily it is an interplay between patient and analyst. It creates an opportunity for the patient's own original and characteristic response to other people to come to the fore with as little interference as possible from subsequently acquired patterns of behaviour.

This relationship with the analyst has frequently been criticized, but it represents something essential to the very nature of psychoanalysis—though only as a transitional stage, and not as an end in itself. The ultimate aim is self-realization, and this is achieved by the patient's breaking away from transference and replacing it by behaviour which corresponds more adequately to his person and situation.

b) Danger of abuses during transference

E.: That may be perfectly correct in principle. But principles are very hard to realize perfectly, and in practice it will depend on whether the analyst carries out treatment according to his professional ethics—in other words, according to these very principles. He may be prudent and very well trained, he may know a lot about the human relationships and childhood impressions of his patient. But ultimately he is only human, and for this reason he is liable—unconsciously, of course, rather than consciously—to try and extend his power by exploiting his relationship with the patient. Priests are familiar with this sort of thing, and pastoral theology has a much longer history to look back over than psychoanalysis. A shadow has fallen over the life of many a priest who could not resist the temptations of such a situation. For centuries warnings have been given against these dangers, and certainly not without success. But we have not been able to eradicate them altogether. And we can certainly do nothing to stop people projecting their feelings or even being genuinely fond of us, and many a priest or teacher has allowed these temptations to get the better of him. Pastoral work requires a priest to be approachable and detached at the same time, and it is difficult to strike the happy medium. And I can well imagine that the danger is just as great for the psychotherapist, perhaps even greater, since his dealings with patients are necessarily much more "intimate". I can envisage very many different forms of getting another person, consciously or unconsciously, "into one's power"; and I am by no means thinking of sexual exploitation alone, though this certainly comes into it. Only a very few defects of the sexual variety need come to the priest's ears to make him very easily suspicious of psychotherapy in general.

M.: The danger of sexual temptations arising when sexual matters are being brought out during transference is probably greater for celibates than for analysts who are married—as they usually are. In fact, I find it rather revealing that it is mainly the theologians who overestimate the danger of sexuality in psychoanalysis, whether for analyst or patient. Many theological arguments remind me of the objections to gynaecological examination brought forward by unmarried women who have remained virgins. These women often look on such an examination as a threat to their chastity, or even to their sexual purity. They are, of course, confusing the anatomical and erotic aspects of their bodies. They have not come to terms with the erotic aspect and are thus ready to sense dangers which do not exist for a person who has experienced "normal love".

E.: I am perfectly prepared to grant that the "celibate outlook" tends very much more easily to magnify dangers in the sexual sphere. This is humanly understandable, though it is a danger in itself for pastoral theology and more attention should be paid to it. All the same, this does not alter the fact that the situation during transference can create difficulties even for the married analyst, and precisely *because* he is married; after all, he has already had sexual experience, which means that his sexual responses will be aroused all the more quickly than those of someone who is (in the positive sense) celibate.

M.: Although I still think you are inclined to lay too much emphasis on "sexual temptations", I will certainly admit that there are dangers of abuse during transference, and psychoanalysts are very well aware of them. Freud himself was concerned mainly with working out the problems of transference during treatment; but in recent years psychoanalytical research has concentrated more intensively on countertransference. This involves the emotions and attitudes which may be dangerous to analyst and patient alike. Indeed, if the analyst does not have his impulses under control he can most certainly fall victim to the dangers of transference. But abuses of the analyst-patient relationship will very seldom be the sort of things which finish up in the courts. Much more frequent and serious than immoral conduct, as well as more difficult to recognize, are things which appear to be perfectly justifiable. For example, if an analyst is in love with one of his women patients, he may well have her in more regularly and for a longer period than he does with less desirable ones; he may be somewhat over-lenient in interpreting her problems, charge her a smaller fee, and all the rest. This is why every prospective psychoanalyst is obliged to undergo a trial analysis. Not only should he experience the psychoanalytical process himself, but he should also be put in a position where he can observe his otherwise almost imperceptible emotional attitudes and bring them better under control. Obviously this affords no absolute guarantee of subsequent professional conduct. A psychotherapist, however well trained, is still human, and his relationship with patients depends very much on his conscience and his moral resources.

c) *Unethical and inadmissible suggestions*

E.: Just like the priest, of course! Nonetheless, I should like to voice another doubt. I have come across cases which gave the impression that the analyst was using the relationship in order to impose his own moral outlook on patients whose ethical convictions happened to be different. The following instance can serve as an illustration. A young woman doctor was undergoing a trial analysis. She was engaged, but had had no sexual intercourse with her fiancé. As a practising Catholic she was of the opinion that intercourse is confined to marriage. During analysis, quite naturally, her relations with her fiancé were brought up, whereupon the analyst kept on and on asking her why she had had no intercourse with this man, although both of them were fully agreed about the marriage. The patient was so indignant at this constant harping that she wanted to break off the analysis.

M.: Did you hear this from the lady herself, or from someone else?

E.: From one of her relatives, a person with plenty of commonsense and not given to exaggeration.

M.: I have a reason for asking this. Descriptions of what goes on during analysis are only too often based on rumour rather than on solid fact. It is a matter of common experience that the farther a rumour travels the more distorted it becomes. Rumours, indeed, are invariably subservient to particular purposes. In a case like this, perhaps, the intention will be to demonstrate the moral questionability of a certain analyst or—as is more likely—of psychoanalysis itself. It is important to mention this, because people's views about psychoanalysis—in Germany at least—are based on rumours and prejudices rather than on factual knowledge.

On the other hand, I can easily imagine an analyst putting such a question to a student or patient. Whether it is relevant or not depends entirely on the individual case, and a distinction will have to be made. Was the question asked because there were indications that it would help the patient to confront certain unconscious inclinations, or was it—as you have assumed on the strength of the account—for the purpose of inducing the patient to have sexual intercourse with her fiancé?

Here, as so often, the significance depends on the motive, and this cannot be determined without more detailed knowledge of the actual case.

E.: If an analyst asks this sort of question to help a patient to come properly to terms with some uncritically accepted piece of morality and turn it into a personal conviction, then there is every justification for it.

But in the case I mentioned it was pretty certainly not for this reason. It would seem that, once a serious personal relationship has been entered into, premarital abstinence is thought of by many psychotherapists as an anachronistic tabu. The analyst here had unhesitatingly expressed his own conviction, probably without any "evil intention" and simply because he took the matter completely for granted. To my mind, the abuse of power during transference is very likely to take this form.

But we are agreed that it is an offence against professional ethics when the analyst gives way to this temptation. At all events, I certainly have no wish to cast aspersions on psychoanalysis on the strength of individual cases.

M.: Your example does, perhaps, touch on other questions of principle. To what extent is it desirable or necessary for a patient to maintain contact with his confessor during analysis? There are two extremes here, and any number of variations in between. In the first case, the patient goes to confession just as he did before taking up analysis. No new problem has arisen as a result of treatment. He confesses everything he finds to be sinful and gets the absolution we cannot give him. In principle, confessions of this sort raise no psychological problems which need be mentioned here. For people like this confession is a sacrament for the purpose of obtaining absolution from things regarded as sinful. Motivation and personal circumstances play a secondary role.

But on the other hand, we are familiar with cases where confession is unconsciously played off against analysis. The penitent, without being asked, tells his confessor that he is undergoing psychoanalytical treatment and asks what he thinks about it. Since, in most cases, the confessor knows very little in detail about the penitent and is not particularly well informed about the meaning or nature of psychoanalysis, he will tend to answer accordingly. His reactions will range from curiosity—"What happens there, then?", to outright condemnation—"You must break it off at once, these analysts tell you to give way to every impulse!" I have never yet heard a patient report a knowledgeable answer from a confessor in cases like this. What the priest really ought to say, in effect, is: "You yourself know why you have decided to go for analysis. I am not familiar with your case or your problems, and I don't know exactly what goes on during analysis." Mind you, if answers of this sort seem to be so rare, it has undoubtedly a lot to do with the patients. When they hurl these questions at the confessor they are hoping unconsciously to find a moral justification for their resistances to analysis, and the sixth commandment can provide a very useful handle.

4. Patient and confessor

M.: The case I have just described may serve to demonstrate another variation of this principle. Some people, deep down, are uncertain about their attitude towards sexual matters—particularly as regards the widespread practice of premarital intercourse which we have already touched on—and they like to get their confessor to give them a sort of certificate of purity and perseverance. Since they are not really convinced, heart and soul, about this matter they want the confessor to give them, as it were, a pat on the back.

This sometimes crops up among Catholic patients, and at bottom it is a means of resisting the responsibility involved in personal judgment and the development of a mature and independent conscience. When resistances like this turn up during analysis great use is made of third parties. Wives tell husbands, children tell parents, girl-friends tell boy-friends—and they all come out with certain details about analytical treatment, with the unconscious intention of getting the other person to support them in their resistance to the analyst or, rather, to analysis itself. In many cases this is very easy, just as easy as in everyday matters. Other people react according to what is said and how it is said—and these reactions will be the ones the patients intend them to have. But since patients are aware of the condition of not discussing details of treatment with others, they will talk about things connected with conscience. This is another way of saying that they agree in principle, but only up to the point where their conscience starts to be involved. And the moment they appeal to conscience all objections are silenced.

What I have just described should make fairly clear what is actually happening. The principle appealed to is perfectly right and proper, but it is being used as a means of resisting personal integration.

E.: If I have understood you rightly there is no serious difference between our views. It is very much to be desired that our confessors should know enough about psychotherapy to be able to work out more or less whether they are being used to further a conscious or unconscious resistance such as you have described.

On the other hand, it is still possible that genuine conscientious misgivings may drive a patient to his confessor, and this opportunity must always be available in principle. We have, of course, already discussed this. Ultimately, psychotherapists and priests alike are equally concerned about mature personal judgment and the moral integration which results from it. *M.:* That this does genuinely involve the problem of self-integration can be seen from another, equally common, occurrence. If a patient voluntarily undergoes therapy and takes it really seriously, it can bring about certain changes in his personal relationships; and the people he lives with may find this hard to get used to, if not actually unacceptable. Thus a young man, twenty-two years old, was starting to become personally self-reliant, but his parents did not think of the new development as independence, but as rebelliousness and obstinacy. In such cases the family quite often try to influence the analyst—"Please get my child to behave properly and respect his parents", and so on. They very often have analysis broken off altogether. Husband, wife or child must correspond to the desired image rather than be what they themselves really wish to be. How far this can be carried may be seen from the following example.

A widow, mother of five children, brought her daughter to me for psychotherapeutic treatment. The daughter was thirty-eight years old and had already been in an institution eleven times. For the last few months she had been lying almost the whole time at home in bed, though she had no physical complaints. She was suffering from jealous illusions, believing that her mother was keeping for herself a lover who in fact did not exist. As therapy went on the patient became more active, left her bed and began to do a bit of housework. The mother was all praise for this successful treatment. A year later I suggested that the daughter should be released from tutelage. At almost every session the patient had been complaining that this tutelage was a painful stigma and that she was always terrified of having to go back to the institution she so much dreaded. The mother complied with this wish, though very reluctantly. And this marked the end of our peaceful relations. She complained that her daughter was now often going for walks on her own, hours on end, without telling her anything about it. This worried her a lot, and her poor old heart couldn't take it. She thought it would be better to have her daughter put under tutelage again. When I would not concur she told me next time, full of indignation, that her daughter had now taken up smoking. She had been checking up occasionally on her handbag and found that cigarettes were missing when she had gone off in the direction of the forest. To prevent a forest-fire the daughter should be sent back to the institution. And in any case she was always "much nicer to live with" when she came back from the institution. When I objected that the patient had become much more self-reliant and independent she retorted that her daughter had even begun to cook for herself and was keeping more and more out of her way. This had never happened before. But she herself was responsible, and it was entirely up to her whether her daughter might continue therapy or not. And the patient did not come again. Four months later she wrote in desperation from an institution, asking to be taken away. The mother had had her sent there on another doctor's recommendation.

The point of this example is that the resistance of other people, too, can play an important role. Here a desire to make one's own image of another person prevail led a mother to have her child put under tutelage. In another case, a patient, whose parents lived in another town, asked anxiously during analysis: "Will my parents love me even when I have been cured?" In this way, relatives often allow someone dependent on them very little chance to become an independent personality. Unconsciously they refuse to accept changes of behaviour, even if these are the result of a more mature and healthy attitude.

Much the same goes for the influence of confessors on their penitents. Often, without noticing it, they admit only certain forms of behaviour as Catholic and treat as un-Catholic and un-Christian everything which does not fit in with their own personal image of a Catholic.

E.: Of course, if a priest acts in this way it is just an all too common lapse into human mediocrity. The aim of the priest, as of the training provided by his Church, is to make human mediocrity correspond rather more nearly to the ideal. Psychotherapy can perform a very useful service here by pointing out certain ways of achieving this which might have passed unnoticed.

In pastoral work it is important to form a much clearer idea of the work which a priest acquainted with the psychotherapist's methods can do in the patient's immediate environment. In many cases he is the very man to help propagate a better understanding of the purpose and methods of psychotherapy. He can help to eliminate unfounded suspicions and misunderstandings, and in particular situations he can also indicate the right way to behave towards a patient or—and this is sometimes even more important—prepare the way for a confidential talk between the family and the analyst. And it is desirable, too, simply because contact will be established between psychotherapist and priest in cases where the patient is a believing Christian.

This brings me to a final question. In such cases, and in general with Catholics who want to undergo psychotherapeutic treatment, is it not important and even indispensable to find a therapist of the same faith?

5. How important is the psychotherapist's own *weltanschauung*?

E.: Any discerning person will agree with you that the first thing to ask is whether a particular analyst is professionally competent and possesses the human qualities which merit confidence. But please do not take it as clerical presumption if a theologian suggests that something further is desirable, something which, I think, is materially relevant. An analyst should be familiar with both the spiritual values and the often very specific mentality of a patient who has grown up in a religious atmosphere, or at least in a particular denominational atmosphere; this is surely important if he is to provide a correct interpretation of certain aspects of transference or resistance, and so on, and understand how significant they are and what personal importance they have for the patient. And I might also add that an analyst should have a certain amount of religious experience of his own, since this particular sphere, more than any other, needs an "inside" appreciation. Quite often in psychotherapeutic literature religious ideas, and ethical ideas based on religion, are dismissed arrogantly and, to my mind, thoughtlessly and superficially as "tabus", and ultimately this may well be because religious phenomena are looked at very much from an outsider's viewpoint and are thus never adequately accounted for.

Moreover, with all regard for the necessary reserve, the analyst will have to intervene in certain crises, either with a prohibition (remember the "bell-glass of denial") or with advice or suggestions. Under certain circumstances the analyst's own creed could be important here.

The personal religious commitment of the psychotherapist may also afford the best protection against psychologism and the short-cut methods of utilitarianism, which are the greatest dangers he is exposed to. The more energetically the analyst devotes himself to the work of helping his patient achieve full integrity of psychic functioning, the greater the risk he runs of seeing only this formal aim, without paying any heed to what really lies behind these aspects of psychic fulfilment. In other words, he is acting—perhaps without realizing it—on the principle that the end justifies the means. I am sorry if this appears rather hackneyed, but the good alone is expedient—the expedient is not necessarily good. Our discussion has already brought out quite clearly that the sensual aspects of psychic health, which are the psychotherapist's principal concern, are subordinate to the reality of spiritual values, particularly the ethical and the religious. If the psychotherapist is personally and vitally committed to these values he will not lose sight of them during his work. I am not trying to say that Catholics should be treated only by Catholic psychotherapists—and genuinely "practising" ones at that—and that Protestants should only go to Protestants, though there is doubtless much to be said for this; but I *should* like to lay down as a minimal requirement that the choice of psychotherapist be based on whether he is a religious person thoroughly familiar with the religious ideas and values to which his patient is committed.

M.: This requirement is perfectly legitimate. One can appreciate that a religious person will be unwilling to co-operate with a psychoanalyst who possesses no organ for the religious element in man. A religious patient may find it very hard to feel the confidence in him which is so necessary for psychoanalysis.

But this principle seems to me somewhat more problematical in practice. How is anyone looking for a psychotherapist to find out whether he is a religious person or not? He will scarcely even know the meaning of all the different terms beginning with "psych"—psychologist, psychiatrist, psychoanalyst, psychotherapist, depth psychologist, and so on. For this reason the Church has resorted in many areas to recommending trustworthy practitioners, or—more accurately —practitioners of the right denomination. To my mind this is very unfortunate, and in some respects even dangerous, because the sense of the religious which you just mentioned is hardly the same thing as membership of a particular denomination. The insistence of many ecclesiastical circles on a religious psychotherapist is simply a faint-hearted caution which reaps its own reward when greater attention is paid to denomination than to medical qualification. This sectarian fear of letting someone of another faith into one's little secrets or of allowing oneself to be seduced from one's own beliefs has encouraged many practitioners to offer their services to a particular denomination. Such practitioners find the confidence of a church body more effective for bringing in the patients than their training and experience. Neither they nor the churches realize the serious damage which can be caused by a doctor-patient relationship based on ideology. They find it much more convenient to pass judgment on cases where a patient has felt himself misunderstood by a psychotherapist of another faith.

When it comes down to practical detail this problem presents much the same sort of difficulties as the attempts to reconcile faith and science. When the churches show an interest in some aspect of this they are inclined to quote "authorities" who fit in with their ideas. Impatient attempts to bridge the gap between religion and science can all too easily obscure the scientific criteria of a particular publication; all that matters is that the opinions or formulations of a particular creed should be confirmed. The churches, of course, are not alone in distorting and misinterpreting scientific discoveries for their own benefit. Convinced atheists are no better. In the solitude of his faith every believer is only too ready to seek out authorized "proofs".

The psychotherapist, too, is affected by this problem. He himself is ultimately a believer in one sense or another, and to that extent I can appreciate your anxiety about the psychotherapist's religious qualifications. The analyst should not use the faith of his patient as a confirmation of his own. This danger is pointed out during training, though not everywhere with equal thoroughness. It is, after all, one aspect of the very complicated phenomenon of counter-transference. How far an individual psychotherapist comes properly to grips with this is always a matter of personal quality and human maturity. Theoretical training, trial analysis and practical experience are very important in helping the practitioner attain to personal and professional integrity, but they can offer no absolute guarantees.

E.: Here I shall bring my questions to an end. Psychotherapy is a wide field and suggests any number of further questions, such as the treatment of individual neurotic symptoms in so far as they touch on ethics and religious life. But our discussion may perhaps have helped to show the level at which the psychotherapist and the priest might work together to everyone's advantage.

III

A Psychotherapist's Queries

Dr Matussek: This will not be the first time a psychoanalyst has sought to analyse and discuss questions of morality, and particularly morality as formulated by the churches. The discussion was set going by Freud himself, and it has not been laid to rest yet. The reason for such interest is obvious: morality and religion are an intrinsic part of human existence and are therefore an object of psychoanalytical research. There are different moralities and different faiths; but this by no means alters the basic fact that every man has a morality and a faith, even if it is an "anti-moralist morality" and an "unbelieving faith".

Freud concerned himself primarily with what is essential and universal in every morality and religion. At that time it was the principle of psychology to explain a phenomenon in terms of the history of its origins, and this led him to investigate the way in which morality and religion might have originated during the course of human development; he assumed that if one wanted to analyse their nature all one would have to do was establish their derivation. In this way he arrived at some very summary definitions of religion and morality, as well as of their three central manifestations—freedom, faith and conscience. But deductions like this are based too much on theoretical generalizations, and they leave the modern scientist cold.

On the other hand, psychoanalysis has turned out to be uncommonly fruitful as a method of investigating moral and

87

religious forms of behaviour and experience. In this particular sector it can also do quite a lot to make moral and religious decisions more personal and to heighten the appreciation of human values.

With any formulated moral system, the Christian included, there is always the danger that the genuinely individual element of personal existence will be left out. This individual element is not a schizoid idiosyncrasy or an exceptional condition, nor is it self-will or a subjective private morality. It is the ability to enter into a personal relationship with another, an ability which is deeply-rooted in human nature and which tends to take more differentiated forms with the development of civilization and culture as well as of the individual himself. To put it in another way, it is the ability to fulfil oneself by responding to what is unique and individual in another. This individual element, which in Christian terms could be described as self-love, is fulfilled by a genuine inward love of one's neighbour, and this, in Christian philosophy, is idential with the love of God.

But this ideal often remains unrealized, and there are any number of different reasons why. Within the limits imposed by this discussion I should like to concentrate especially on what psychoanalysis means when it talks of a belief turning into an ideology.

Outside the specialist vocabulary of the psychologists ideology is understood principally in the sociological sense. The social sciences deal with the socially relevant ideologies, such as Communism, Socialism, Liberalism, to mention only a few political ones. That something may become an ideology in the psychological sense, too, is seldom if ever appreciated. Ideological behaviour *may* take the form of a social ideology, but not necessarily. Any faith or set of values can be lived ideologically.

And Christian teaching is no exception. For one man it

may be the object of a faith based on deep conviction, for another it may be simply an ideology. Indeed, it may be said that ideological attitudes among preachers and people alike have been, and still are, more widespread in the Christian world than has hitherto been admitted. There is even a good deal to support the view that, from the moment Christianity became a world religion, ideological attitudes to faith and ideological means of spreading it have, for a great diversity of historical reasons, been much more prominent than the ideal of personal fulfilment contained in principle in the New Testament. For the New Testament emphasized freedom (of the children of God from the "law"), conscience and interiorization as the constituent elements of faith—in other words, the very things which distinguish faith from ideology.

In *The Future of an Illusion*, Freud prophesied the end of all religions and expressed the opinion that, as time went on, people would abandon the collective neurosis of religion in favour of unvarnished reality. This would, admittedly, make man as lonely as a child which has left its father's house, but it would also make him fundamentally more honest. Nowadays we can see that this prophecy was itself based on an ideological concept of reality, since neither reality in its entirety, nor the ultimate meaningfulness of reality, are things which can be grasped by science.

But Freud's prognosis does appear to contain something which we can still accept as valid today, and this is the process of transformation in which the Christian religion now finds itself. It is usual to describe it as an adaptation to the modern world, though this really touches only one external aspect of the matter. More decisive is the internal aspect, which can be described as a transition from ideology to faith and is, in fact, very often necessary for the average run of Christians.

This process is of its very nature a crisis. Ideological attitudes, after all, have the advantage of making faith easier, though they also have the disadvantage of leading one away from reality, particularly from the reality of one's fellow-men—and thus from religious reality in the Christian sense. For this reason the questions I am going to put to you as the moral theologian, and the misgivings I want to voice, revolve mainly round matters connected in some way or other with the theme of "ideology, faith and conscience".

Fr Egenter: I agree with you that the way in which the Christian religion has been propagated and developed over the centuries has quite often led to faith being turned into ideology, without Christians as a whole ever being properly aware of the fact. A theologian, therefore, should be grateful to psychotherapy if it draws attention to the criteria by which the cause of this process can be discerned; with the methods at its disposal it is certainly in a better position to do this than our usual pastoral psychology. It can make it all the easier for us to see what our pastoral work is really about and show us the best way to set about re-examining our moral and pastoral doctrine—a duty which is always with us. On the other hand, the psychotherapist will be doing himself a good turn if, in the course of his work, he looks beyond the abundant and all-too-natural defects of average Catholic morality and piety and tries to gain an insight into the problems and methods of present-day moral theology, even though the results may not be fully felt for a generation or more to come.

Before we go on to this part of our discussion I should like to make quite clear that there is no intention here of providing anything like a comprehensive defence, or even an account, of the pastoral situation and its abuses. Justification of the past, and even critical appraisal of the present, must be restricted to the minimum needed to help psychotherapists and priests work together in mutual understanding.

1. The moral assumptions of the average Catholic

M.: I should like to start with something which is often met with among Catholic patients during psychoanalytical treatment. They feel and think themselves to be Catholics and Christians mainly because they observe certain commands and regulations. They go to church on Sundays, eat no meat on Friday, say their prayers regularly, receive the sacraments more or less frequently, try to remain "pure" before marriage, steer clear of adultery after marriage, and use no birth-control methods. The children are sent to Catholic schools. They shun films and reading-matter which have been declared questionable in clerical quarters. And quite often they will take it for granted as Catholics that they will vote for a particular political party, especially in country districts.

The principle governing this idea of the faith is that a person is a good Catholic and Christian if these and other characteristic acts are duly carried out. People are Catholic or Christian, not because they love more deeply, show greater forbearance or are more concerned to do justice to their fellow-men, but because they perform certain acts—even if these should leave the heart untouched. Such an attitude lacks the deep conviction which would enable them to get to the heart of other people and thus to come to know themselves better. So it is hardly surprising that, as far as moral substance is concerned, there is very little real difference between them and non-Catholics or non-Christians. They take advantage of others, wish them ill, have no deeper and more personal love for their spouses and do no more justice to the claims of their children, and all this quite apart from the obligation to love their enemies, which features so prominently in the Sermon on the Mount.

Patients whose Christian lives are primarily a set of external criteria are generally quite unmoved when an analyst tries to suggest that this is moral short-sightedness. They are often well primed with arguments they have obviously learned in the course of religious instruction. They will point out that we are all sinners and can never overcome our sinfulness, or they will dismiss the problem by saying that faith cannot alter human nature and all its weaknesses.

I have the impression that this state of affairs does not apply merely to individual cases I myself have come across. It seems to me much more likely that it is a deeply-rooted characteristic of faith and morality as understood by a large number of people, and that it can be found in one form or another in all the Christian churches—the emphases will obviously differ. What is psychologically so remarkable here is the impossibility of distinguishing between the morality of Christians and non-Christians, except, of course, for the purely external criteria; and this is particularly striking when one compares the utterly different motivations. The Christians are concerned ultimately with the eternal salvation (or perdition) which will follow upon the moral quality of their lives, while the non-Christians are concerned merely to fulfil themselves here on earth, without any thought for consequences in a world to come. It might surely be expected that those who have more to win or lose would be leading a deeper and more honest moral life. In your opinion, would it be far from the truth to say that there is very little moral difference between Catholics, non-Catholics and non-Christians, apart, of course, from the external criteria?

E.: The old catchphrase "Catholics are no better than any others" is probably quite true if you think of the enormous mass of people who have been baptized and who pay their Church taxes. The times are long past when the early Christian writer of the *Epistle to Diognetus* could say:

> Christians do not differ from other men either in nation or in language and customs. . . . They adapt themselves

to the country's customs in dress, food and their whole manner of living, but in all this they manifest a wonderful and, as everyone will tell, a surprising transformation in their lives as citizens. . . . They dwell on earth, but their conversation is in heaven. They obey the laws in force, and in their way of life they go even further than the laws require. They love everyone and yet are persecuted by everyone. . . . They are poor and yet make many rich, they are provoked by others and yet give their blessing, they are derided and yet pay respect. They do good, but are punished as evildoers. . . . In short, as the soul is in the body, so are Christians in the world.

We who belong to a world-wide Church, looking back as it does over centuries of secularization in the course of the development of Christian civilization, will simply have to face the fact that any comparison with the life of the primitive Christian churches places us in a very bad light. We do not, of course, have to look very far before extenuating reasons come to hand. For instance, we can point to the universal historical fact that charismatic movements gradually lose their substance and vitality as they become more widespread and institutionalized; each of us, as Leopold von Ranke said, has his "immediate relationship with God", and an abundance of grace flows down to each of us from the cross of Christ according to the measure of our personal faith.

On the other hand, to suggest that the moral substance of Christians and non-Christians is indistinguishable is rather a sweeping judgment, and it both can and must be accepted with certain reservations. Enquiries, for example, have shown that in parishes where the priest carries out an intelligible liturgy, properly conducted and explained, instead of just going through the Latin prayers on his own at the altar, the number of men who go to church, especially from among the workers, rises considerably—as does also the willingness of families to have children. This is an indication that genuine moral and religious energies are often just below the surface waiting to be tapped. And it is impossible to assess how far the moral standards—and even the general human level—of the population as a whole would go down were it not for the ordinary people who inconspicuously lead a Christian life from their very hearts and whose behaviour in everyday life leaves its own mark. But the fact still remains: as far as the vast bulk of nominal Catholics is concerned you are perfectly right.

M.: Is this, in your opinion, simply something which has to be taken for granted in view of the fragility of human nature, or do you see the externalized faith and morality I have alluded to as a problem for moral theology?

E.: As a problem for moral theology, without any doubt whatsoever. In fact, it is one of the most urgent problems we are confronted with today. The roots of the evil which we have come to call legalism reach far into the past. I should like, if I may, to delve into history at this point, for otherwise it will be impossible to make it clear why matters cannot be mended overnight.

The trend towards legalism began, basically, as early as the Christianization of the young Germanic nations. The missionaries at that time were monks, and their task was to impress the major moral obligations in the simplest possible form upon people who could neither read nor write. And for a long time these newly Christianized lands were served by a pastoral clergy whose theological training could at best be described as modest. The monks, therefore, took the disciplinary system of their religious life, which included penitential taxes for individual offences against the monastery regulations, and applied it to their pastoral work among the Christian people. The early medieval "Penitential Books" drew up lists of duties and sins and frequently prescribed appropriate penances. In this way the people came to assess their moral and religious life in terms of individual "do's and don'ts". This does not mean that no one at that time had any real grasp of the Christian ethos or of heartfelt spirituality. But the ascetic and religious writings on the subject were unable to have anything like the same widespread influence as the penitential practice. Things gradually improved: the moral education and religious life of the pastoral clergy and then of the people became deeper. During the high Middle Ages, for example, the classical moral theology of Thomas Aquinas was based on the virtues and aimed at inculcating a morality founded on personal conviction. But with the decline of the Middle Ages scholasticism degenerated into nominalism, which denied the possibility of deriving ethical norms from essential nature. As a result, formal precepts and legalistic obedience came more strongly to the fore again.

There is no need to follow up this development in any further detail. At all events, the text-books of moral theology became principally manuals for confessors, and remained so until very recently. Although they contained much that was genuinely ethical, they also included an enormous amount of legal material, and thus directed attention overwhelmingly to legal behaviour. The so-called "duties of one's state of life", consisting of individual acts which could be listed and weighed up, such as Sunday Mass, paying taxes, keeping contracts and so on, came to receive more emphasis than the fundamental commands of greater essential importance for Christian life, such as humility, honesty, and personal faith, hope and charity.

Moral theology today is trying to move towards a morality based on genuine Christian conviction. But there can be no question of despising laws and commandments. These are indispensable aids in that they establish the "moral minimum" below which any life in God's grace is impossible; and with

E

their detailed indications they act as a sort of signpost towards a genuinely human and Christian life. But Christian morality can never rest content with mere fences and signposts. Laws and prescriptions must never be allowed to obscure the underlying values which they are designed to protect and promote. Civic duties should not be fulfilled merely because they have laws and sanctions attached to them; they should be seen as providing a means whereby we can realize the dignity and vital importance of the civic community, as well as of the commonweal in which we all have a share. We should not give alms or help our neighbour simply because such conduct is presented as a duty in some "examination of conscience before confession", but because we personally acknowledge another's need of our help and are prepared to express our good-will in practical action.

In this effort to work out a Christian morality based on inward conviction psychotherapy affords us very welcome assistance. I do not mean simply that it overcomes the neurotic barriers which prevent a patient from leading a personally meaningful moral life. I also mean that by doing this—and also by making its work known to wider circles—it directs even "healthy" people's attention to the need for a fully developed adult conscience. But there can be no question of this happening so long as people are unable to do without the crutches of legalistic obedience and experience their moral life as something "meaningful" and "personal".

M.: Although I am perfectly ready to acknowledge that theologians and psychotherapists are aiming at the same thing in this matter, I am afraid I shall have to come back once more to the brute reality which psychotherapists find themselves up against in practice. Our professional concern is not with the debate among the theologians but with the practising Christian. And time and again we find that the attitude of the practising Christian is a solid block of externalized legalism.

The fault lies, surely, in the methods of religious and moral instruction?

E.: Present practice in such instruction I can judge only superficially. The point of greatest interest for the moral theologian is the way this usually reflects the sort of theological training which the priest himself has received, whether recently or somewhat farther back. It may seem a very general remark, but it is important to point out that there are a number of difficulties here for our discussion. You have had your own experiences as far as pastoral practice is concerned; but you will be referring to a form of theological thinking which in many ways has been superseded. It is evident that if theological scholars and teachers are doing their work properly they will always be several steps ahead of what is going on in practice. I think our discussion will quite often reveal that the moral theology at present being taught in our seminaries is already taking into account many of the things about which you are concerned.

On the other hand, when you come out with your objections and misgivings you will certainly not be tilting at windmills; after all, a psychotherapist is concerned with things as he finds them in his professional work. As I have suggested, practice very often lags behind, and this will become all the more apparent since our discussion will be revolving not merely around individual questions and isolated cases but around fundamental facts and tendencies in the general Christian attitude to life—and, as everyone knows, changes come about more slowly here than among the theorists.

But to return to your question! I should like to state first that the attitudes you come up against are due only to a limited extent to the instruction given by the Church. The majority of nominal Catholics are, practically, almost unaffected by this instruction. To the extent that a Catholic is still "practising" he will rest content with fulfilling certain minimal requirements, expressed in tangible items like Easter duties, "attendance" at Sunday Mass and the like.

M.: When I mentioned externalized Christianity I was not referring primarily to nominal Christians as you are now. Christians of this sort would, for example, hardly abide by the prohibition placed on the use of contraceptives. I was referring to certain "law-abiding" people who think of themselves as good Christians. Their assertion that they would never lay any claim to be good Christians is just a turn of phrase which has very little to do with their actual conduct. These are people with a sense of religious superiority, a willingness to judge and condemn, a short-sighted partisan religion which allows no one else any scope for thinking and acting differently, and—it need hardly be said—an ostentatious love of neighbour which eases their own consciences and falls far short of its object.

To avoid all suspicion that we are using unsuitable examples we might concentrate our attention on the priests—men, in other words, who can most certainly not be called nominal Christians in the usual sense. At all events, they pay much more active heed to the prevailing regulations and instructions for spiritual and religious life than do average Christians. But how is it that these men, who are constantly in close contact with religious things, do not appear to be any more moral or even religious than the bulk of nominal Christians? You have only to think of the widespread complaints among the general public about so many of the sermons given, where the fervour is skin-deep, or where the priest seems to be enjoying the sound of his own voice or to be talking like a teacher who always knows best. Obviously, the sermon is only one criterion among many others—but it is a very important one as far as the Christian public is concerned. As many enquiries have shown, it enables people to form a fairly shrewd estimate of religious quality. The usual excuse, that it is impossible to be at the top of one's form Sunday after Sunday, reveals ultimately nothing much more than the tendency to confuse religious insipidity with rhetorical condition.

E.: But it must be remembered that we priests are, in the first place, just plain Christians; we do not remain unaffected by the prevailing mentality, and we are threatened by the spirit of legalism just as much as other Christians. Our vocational work and our lives as priests are governed by any number of ecclesiastical regulations. Our training, too, has taken place mostly in the well-ordered atmosphere of boarding-school and seminary, and here, also, there are many "duties" which help to foster legalism and all the dangers this has for personal religious conviction. Thus it is not only the theological instruction itself which plays a part here. The important factor is whether and to what extent an individual priest, given these circumstances, has managed to integrate his personal life in a genuinely religious way. This is just as important as doctrinal content if a sermon is to have any power of conviction.

I will certainly grant you that our preaching leaves much to be desired, and, particularly, that theological training in the past has underestimated the dangers of legalism. There are reasons which make this understandable and even excuse it to some extent, but these I shall leave aside. At all events, many laypeople genuinely interested in religion do complain that the preaching contains little religious meat and that it is addressed too little to responsible adult consciences. But there is a fairly general awareness of what needs to be done. The new German catechism is based on the idea of individual conscience and suggests many practical ways of helping a sense of values to develop. And again, one result of the present liturgical revival has been the reintroduction of the homily, which is essentially an explanation of the biblical texts in the liturgy of the day—and where this takes place it will be found that casuistic moral instruction gives way to the biblical ethos, which is not legalistic at all.

2. The different ways the bible can be used in the formation of Christian values

M.: You mention the biblical ethos, and this gives me the cue for another question. In so far as the biblical ethos plays any part in the Church's preaching it would appear to be presented very one-sidedly. Only as regards certain norms is the bible abundantly quoted as evidence that the Church's attitude could under no circumstances be different—for, after all, a divine commandment is at issue. But other norms—which have been set forth just as explicitly in the bible—are not taught, or practised, with quite the same consistency. There are several places in the Sermon on the Mount which reveal this tendency, and a single example may suffice.

Of the many precepts contained in the Sermon on the Mount, it is mainly those concerning marriage which are declared as divine commands. The Church is very ready to emphasize the uncompromising rejection of divorce and constantly quotes Matthew 5:32—"Every one who divorces his wife, except on the ground of unchastity, makes her an adulteress; and whoever marries a divorced woman commits adultery."

But the Sermon on the Mount also contains the command to love our enemies. Now it might have been imagined that the Church would have stressed this precept just as forcefully as the indissolubility of marriage. It might then have been possible to forbid every Christian to indulge in any sort of hostility towards his enemies, and to back this up as a matter of course by saying that it is not for us to dispute the point, since God has so decreed.

Do you see any contradiction here in the Church's attitude? How is it that the Sermon on the Mount has been used so inconsistently in the formation of Christian values?

E.: We might, perhaps, not confine the question to the Sermon on the Mount but take the New Testament as a whole; after all, the Church's teaching on marriage is based not so much on Matthew 5:32 as on other passages outside the Sermon on the Mount (*Matt.* 19:3 ff.; 1 *Cor.* 7:1 ff.; *Eph.* 5:21 ff., etc.). And the New Testament, taken as a whole, hardly implies that the command to love one's enemies absolutely forbids all "hostility" whatsoever, such as a defensive war or the use of force against a malefactor.

M.: I am not trying to suggest that the morality of Catholic marriage is based exclusively on that one particular passage of scripture. What I *am* trying to say is that some of the precepts of the Sermon on the Mount have found their way into the Christian sense of values, while others have not. Take these words: "If you are offering your gift at the altar, and there remember that your brother has something against you, leave your gift there before the altar and go; first be reconciled to your brother, and then come and offer your gift" (*Matt.* 5:23-4). Or again: "But woe to you that are rich, for you have received your consolation" (*Luke* 6:24).

And yet the passages I have mentioned concerning marriage, and others like them, have been taught so explicitly that they have penetrated into the system of values of Christians with no more than a routine religious education.

Furthermore, what you have said about the command to love one's enemies does not seem to me to give an adequate account of the system of values actually prevailing in ecclesiastical circles. Our recent past has furnished examples enough. The command to love our enemies may not exclude "legitimate defensive wars", but it most certainly does exclude wars of aggression. We have just had one. But I myself never heard of any priest or bishop who made a public protest against Hitler's wars. Nor were Christians ever warned not to take part in them because to do so would be an offence against a divine precept. On the contrary: some bishops actually admonished Catholic soldiers "to do their duty in obedience to the Führer and be ready to sacrifice their whole individuality". Yet the bishops protested publicly against the sterilization laws of the Nazi regime and forbade Catholics to allow themselves to be sterilized—characteristically with occasional allusions to the fact that a person who had been sterilized could enjoy sexual intercourse for pleasure only, without any consideration of "possible consequences".

I am not bringing this up for the sake of analysing our recent past. My only concern is to show that the values on which Christians—priests included—base their attitudes in practice are determined less by the ethos of the bible than by historical and psychological factors which are not always fully recognized for what they are.

E.: That is not to be denied. The Church cannot claim infallibility or perfection in its pastoral activity, and has no intention of doing so. We have, in other words, to reckon with human error, and many of us older priests, for instance, will have to reproach ourselves for keeping silent too much under the Third Reich.

It is true that the Church does preach some biblical precepts more emphatically than others, but there are objective reasons for this. The scriptures certainly apply to all men and to all ages; but the emphasis placed on individual precepts varies according to times and circumstances. For instance, the morality of a nation will tend to decline in the later stages of a cultural epoch, and it is then necessary to be more thorough and emphatic about the basic norms of Christian marriage.

It is also important to bear in mind the distinction between the fundamental precepts and the detailed instructions regarding one's state of life, to which we have already referred, as well as that between prohibitions and positive commands. Pastorally speaking, stricter emphasis will have to be placed on the things which are absolutely indispensable for a life in God's grace than on those which go well beyond the "moral minimum" and lead to greater maturity and fulfilment in Christian living. And another reason for the uneven emphasis on biblical precepts is that one commandment may be of vital importance for the ecclesiastical community (for example, the celebration of the eucharist by the New Testament people of God), while other biblical instructions are more of an appeal to the freedom and magnanimity of the individual Christian (such as the duty to give alms), or are influenced by the competing claims of other norms in one and the same situation (such as when love of one's enemy clashes with the obligation to defend one's professional or family reputation). When it comes to individual cases it is necessary to take a closer look.

M.: What interests the psychotherapist most of all is human error, particularly at the unconscious level. Ever since psychoanalysis first appeared on the scene we have come to realize more clearly than before that the subjective hierarchy of values in an individual's life is determined to some extent by the individual's own personality. There is no such thing as a sense of values independent of the individual personality. A person's own life history, internal and external, goes into the formation of a set of values, and in the same way the particular historical period will see to it that, at certain times and in certain places, priority is given to some values at the expense of others.

In this connection our interest is not so much in the historical reasons behind the changes in perspective—which moral theologians acknowledge anyway—as in the dependence of values on the individual personality. Psychoanalysis has taught us that unconscious forces go into the making of a sense of values and of moral behaviour in practice, even if they are not the direct causes of them. Thus, with certain types of people we will find priority given to values such as property, justice and purity. In one case these values will be at the top of the scale, while in another the equivalent trio might be self-effacement, self-sacrifice and suffering.

Now, much too much importance has been attached to sins in the sexual sphere, and not for the first time in the nineteenth century. Would you be prepared to admit that this has happened, to some extent at least, because theologians—who are, after all, one of the factors in the formation of Christian values among the faithful—are almost without exception celibate? Here is a group of men for whom sexuality is predominantly something forbidden, illicit, and to be kept at arm's length.

If the Church emphasizes the biblical ethos as regards conjugal matters much more forcefully and effectively than as regards love of enemy, power and riches, might this not be bound up, at least in part, with the celibate morality of the priesthood?

E.: The fact that the Church proclaims the word through celibates is not of itself a sufficient explanation of the great emphasis laid on sexual morality, and particularly not of the specifically negative and prohibitive approach to it. Quite apart from the objective importance of sexual norms for the continued existence of a nation, there is also the consideration that, as early as the first Christian centuries, a number of influences hostile to sexuality crept in from the world of antiquity, and they probably made themselves just as much felt in the Eastern Church, where priests are married.

But so long as this is borne in mind I am quite prepared to agree with you. It is both good and necessary to remind celibates of the danger inherent in their own particular way of life. It would be rather malicious to dismiss the recurrent over-emphasis on conjugal morality as nothing more than the revenge taken by celibates, though sub-conscious resentment may play some part in individual cases. The danger must be understood in the sense you have indicated. Where the sexual sphere is experienced only as something to be kept at arm's length, the aspect of moral danger will be seen much more clearly; not because there is anything reprehensible about it, but because sexual activity has been offered up as a religious sacrifice to God. The natural sexual urges remain active even among celibates. The celibate will experience them first and foremost as dangers; their positive value may be something he knows only in theory, and even then not always adequately. The aspects which affect one immediately will always occupy one's interest, and from the fullness of the heart the mouth speaks, even in the pulpit.

For this reason, the over-emphasis on sexual morality which appeared, if not for the first time, then at least most unmistakably, during the nineteenth century can only be put in proper perspective within the Christian ethos as a whole if special care is taken to see that future priests both understand and experience their sexuality as something at once personal and supra-personal. This does not mean, of course, that the prospective celibate should gain first-hand sexual experiences before he decides on the celibacy of the priesthood. What he absolutely must realize, and not just theoretically, is that the awakening of the sexual urges—for the future priest as for everyone else—is a development which draws a person out of the cocoon of his own individual being and can make him conscious both of the necessity of entering into a dialogue with another person and of the many possibilities this opens up for him. In his sacrifice of marriage "for the sake of the kingdom of heaven", the Catholic priest will try to base his decision on good theological grounds and to live up to it as honestly as he can. And the real reason why he should experience all this in his own person is that a partner of the other sex is supremely important for the dialogue of human living, and this importance is not confined simply to marriage and personal sexuality. This fact must be taken into account both in the training we receive and in the training we try to give ourselves. Today this is realized clearly enough in the training of priests, though not everywhere. All successful atempts to fill in the gaps here will be reflected in the general atmosphere of the Church's methods of moral instruction.

3. Psychological dangers in the prevailing idea of grace

M.: All the Christian churches are familiar with grace and its relationship with the work of Christ, but they differ in the way they interpret man's sharing in it. The Catholic Christian, unlike others, believes himself to be in possession of a special fullness of grace which is given to him in a specific way through the seven sacraments. As a result of the religious instruction he has received the individual believer thinks of this as an exceedingly powerful stream of grace pouring down upon him through the sacraments. Since grace is so intimately bound up with the external signs, the Church commends the frequent reception of the sacraments as the surest way of attaining to the perfection of moral life.

Among Catholic patients, therefore, it is not uncommon to find the idea that if they receive the sacraments regularly they will become morally perfect even to the point of "offering up their whole lives", though they will know, of course, that they have to play their own part if grace is to be effective. But neither the consciousness of a more abundant share in sacramental grace nor the moral endeavour undoubtedly present in many cases makes these people any better. Ethically it is impossible to distinguish them from others whose moral exertions are just as great. And it might even be that frequent reception of the sacraments will bar the way to moral maturity. Even where a considerable degree of moral endeavour is involved all expectation tends to be concentrated on help from above, and no progress is made.

It is typical of people like this that they measure their spiritual maturity in terms of rigorously selected virtues or vices. They will then take one or more vices and try to eradicate them with the aid of the sacraments—frequent confession, for instance. A simple example of this alternation between sin and the struggle against sin through receiving the sacraments is the attitude towards masturbation or similar acts designated as sinful. People will often think of themselves as polluted by one particular sin, though pure in all other respects. The sin is not experienced in terms of its underlying causes but as an offence against God, as separation from the Creator, as a transgression against all that is holy, and so on. And it is believed that all that is needed to obtain the desired moral victory is frequent contact with Christ in the sacrament.

If such people come for psychotherapy (and their attitude to God and grace makes this a comparatively rare event), the analyst finds himself up against considerable difficulties. These difficulties arise because they think of grace as the most efficacious remedy against sin, and also because they are so preoccupied with self-gratification and suchlike acts that they are unable to experience anything else properly as a sin. Self-centredness, inability to make genuine contact with others, hidden aggressions, spiritual complacency and all the other features typical of these cases will be realized at best with the mind alone. There will seldom be any deep feeling or conviction about them.

The question I should like to put, then, is this: is it not true that the concepts and images by which the Catholic doctrine of grace is made known positively encourage this mistaken religious behaviour among people with a strict Catholic education?

E.: Before I go into your question I should like to say a word about the observations you have just made. The regular and proper reception of the sacraments can most certainly lead to greater moral and religious maturity and the practice is definitely to be encouraged; this is something to which all Catholic Christians will hold firmly. But I would hardly venture to assert that Christians who act in this way do not become morally better; on the contrary, pastoral priests can point to any number of heartening results. You may, of course, be right in saying that in some cases, and even, if you like, in many cases these enthusiastic receivers of the sacraments do not become any better, to the outward eye at least. But only God can pass a fitting judgment here. We ourselves must form our ideas with extreme caution, and we shall have to draw distinctions in individual cases.

It is possible, for instance, that a person may only *seem* not to be getting any better. The physical and psychical predispositions may be so unfavourable that he simply cannot overcome his "besetting sin"; for example, his irascibility or jealousy may bring him into conflict with his environment for the whole of his life. Nonetheless, it is also possible that the external failure itself may be causing him to grow spiritually and to accept himself with all his weaknesses; in this way he may come increasingly to learn the ultimate Christian wisdom, which is the humble recognition that however indispensable our own human endeavour may be it will always remain an empty shell, and that all things must be hoped for ultimately as a gift of God's grace. In post-war literature there has been a special predilection for these borderline Christians; you have only to think of Graham Greene's whisky-priest.

But it is possible that frequent reception of the sacraments may—to all appearances—have effected no real improvement. One reason for this may be a false idea of the way the sacraments function, a point I shall be coming back to. And sacramental practice can also be influenced by social and environmental considerations and carried out perfunctorily, without any genuine personal commitment.

Again, it may also be that a sort of subconscious "engineering" is taking place. A young man may, for example, fail to overcome a "habitual sin" of self-gratification because, deep down, he is trying to avoid making a final decision as to marriage or the priesthood. "I must overcome this sin before making any decision." Here the sin is being subconsciously encouraged for the sake of some unacknowledged purpose. The examples you have given would seem to suggest something along these lines. It may well be that the "improvement" sets in very quickly once some circumstance or other has made the dreaded decision easier. But it is also possible that the person concerned must first undergo a radical "metanoia", which means a fundamental re-thinking of his whole situation, or a conversion affecting the very depths of his being. In many cases this will never be achieved without the help of the psychotherapist. I am suggesting all these possibilities because it is important to remember that each case must be taken individually.

And now for your question as to the way the Church presents its doctrine of grace. In individual cases, and even throughout whole historical periods, this can obviously leave a lot to be desired. I will mention only the indulgence sermons of the late Middle Ages and the anger these aroused in Martin Luther. Again, if the Catholic idea of grace is less than perfectly satisfactory, not to say egocentric, it is probably due very largely to modern individualism, which did not call a halt at the religious sphere.

In general, one might say that there are three main reasons for unfruitful sacramental practice on the part of individual Catholics. First, when the sacraments are thought of too materially, so that people expect a sort of gift-parcel of grace, all duly entered in the celestial accounts-book, as a reward for moral endeavour, and are much more interested in this aspect than in the effective influence of the sacraments upon moral and religious life. Secondly, when faulty instruction has allowed magical ideas to take over, so that people expect the external performance alone to have an absolutely guaranteed effect regardless of the personal co-operation of the receiver. And thirdly, when people become "liturgically-minded" and sacramentalist; they may try to carry out the sacramental and cultic acts with all moral and religious seriousness, not just for aesthetic reasons, and yet turn their attention away from the duties of the Christian in the world and forget the importance of proving their moral worth in everyday life.

I do not think that our modern methods of presenting sacramental life are blatantly unsatisfactory, though the theological training and personal religious maturity of individual preachers and catechists may often result in a certain measure of deviation from the ideal. I would even say that a very desirable change seems to be taking place in the theology of grace and the sacraments. "Grace and nature" is giving way to "grace and person". People will thus be less inclined to concentrate on grace as a help expected for moral and religious life and will no longer look on the sacrament primarily as a "means of grace"; they will come to see each of the sacraments as a particular form of encounter with the glorified Christ and to appreciate their purpose and value in terms of further religious ends. Once sacramental piety has been purified and deepened in this way for the individual Christian the effects on his moral life will be greatly increased. Among the psychically healthy a sacramental practice of this sort would hardly bar the way to moral maturity.

M.: But here again, what concerns me is the actual psychotherapeutic situation. It is impossible to wait until personal sacramental piety is securely established. With individual Catholic patients we will have to go on reckoning with an unsatisfactory sacramental practice which acts as a hindrance, or even as a total barrier, to moral maturity. I shall have to put another question. How is the confessor or the person affected to recognize that moral development is being impeded by a false religious attitude, particularly as regards the concept of grace?

E.: In general I would say that if a Christian thinks less of grace and gifts of grace and more of God himself, and remembers that God is graciously and mercifully disposed to us and lovingly calls upon us, he will then be in a better position to hope that his own response in the sacramental encounter with God will assist rather than impede the process of moral development.

In special cases where the struggle against a particular sin has come very much to the fore, the person affected, with the help of his confessor, will have first of all to find out how this conspicuous defect, which may well be obscuring all other considerations, compares with the rest of his moral behaviour. If the general level of behaviour in other respects is high, and if there is reason to suppose that the person is "tearing himself to pieces" with anxiety, a priest who has learnt the lessons of psychotherapy will treat it as a neurotic symptom which does not allow of any immediate judgment as to subjective sinfulness. If confidence at this point were to be placed simply in frequent reception of the sacraments and the working of grace, sacramental practice could easily turn into a brake on psychic healing and, consequently, on moral development; it could also lead to an inadequate idea of grace and the way it works through the sacraments. In this case attention would have to be turned to the natural bases of moral and religious life, as well as to the fact that healthy sacramental piety, and ultimately greater moral maturity, will be impossible unless something is done to tackle the psychic disturbances which took place at a stage prior to moral responsibility.

M.: This seems to me to be an important point of contact between moral theology and psychotherapy. No moral teaching, not even that of the Catholic Church with its particular emphasis on the outward signs of grace, can afford to neglect the natural bases of moral behaviour. *Gratia supponit naturam*—grace presupposes nature; this has always been carefully pointed out in theory, as, for that matter, have most rational principles. In practice, however, things have often been otherwise. As regards moral behaviour theologians have acted, and still do act, as though the psychological basis of ethical life has been fully accounted for and needs no further empirical research. Thus even today, they still make frequent appeal to Thomas Aquinas and other Doctors of the Church in matters of psychology and are much given to talking about the centuries-old psychological wisdom of Holy Mother Church. This complacent insistence on traditional solutions often blinds them to the need for expert studies; and in so far as these studies are psychological they must be left to the secular sciences.

E.: Modern theologians are acutely aware of this objection and have taken it to heart. We realize full well, especially as regards psychology, that the metaphysical theses of the scholastics will have to be corrected and amplified by the findings of empirical psychology, particularly hermeneutic psychology.

M.: On the whole I do not think that hermeneutic psychology provides the best help; there is always a danger of its becoming too subjective. But as far as psychoanalysis is concerned, this method enables us to a very large extent to carry out accurate observations of the course of personal development even in the moral sphere. Whether the information obtained in this way will always be used correctly when it comes to forming theories is a secondary question, and it by no means affects the value of this method for observing the many complex factors which influence the course of individual development. All success in this direction will give us valuable information about the phenomenon of conscience.

4. Ecclesiastical measures for protecting faith and morals

M.: I have already mentioned that the ideas many Catholics have about faith and morality are centred more around external acts than around personal intentions and attitudes, which are ethically of greater relevance. A concrete instance may help to set this more clearly in focus.

A woman patient, forty years old, wanted to read one of the books of Jean-Paul Sartre. She was a Catholic and asked me whether she ought to read it. I said it was up to her. She then expressly indicated that she wanted to read it out of philosophical interest and not for any reason connected with her work. She also asked me whether she ought to consult a priest and obtain permission. I did not think this necessary and told her so.

Would a moral theologian say I had acted rightly?

E.: I should like to counter this with another question. Would a psychoanalyst say you had acted rightly? In my opinion your answer was a departure from the reserve expected of the psychotherapist and was coloured by your own personal views.

M.: My reply was not coloured by my own views. And it was based on a fairly thorough familiarity with the case. And anyway, the psychoanalyst's rule of abstinence does not mean that personal opinions may not be expressed in any situation or under any circumstances. In fact, they occasionally serve the purpose of helping the patient to make his own decisions for himself, and this includes the possibility of his disagreeing with the analyst.

E.: As regards the actual case itself, the patient would have been obliged by Church law as then in force to obtain permission to read the book. The writings of Sartre do not merely contain occasional errors or anti-ecclesiastical out-bursts; they deliberately attack the faith and moral teaching of the Catholic Church. Works like this fall under the heading of prohibited books, and reading them renders a person liable to excommunication.

Now, it is no secret that the Church's present legislation regarding books is not altogether adapted to the modern situation, and a change is anticipated. In its present form it may quite often be a hindrance to the growth and exercise of Christian conscience, although a person with an educated conscience will in many cases be able to resort to what is known as *epikia,* which means that he will claim the freedom to act against the letter of the law whenever there is any serious reason for assuming that the legislator would not reasonably have intended a binding obligation in particular circumstances.

The question of the Church's legislation concerning books raises the fundamental problem of the relationship between ecclesiastical authority and the individual conscience. This problem will doubtless mean very little to those who have no time for ecclesiastical authority. But if a Catholic is ready to take the Church's position into account and subject it to informed and dispassionate analysis, his criticism will provide the Church with very useful help in its dialogue with the world and facilitate what John XXIII called the "aggiornamento", or adaptation to modern life, which would be beneficial to Church and world alike.

The reason behind these laws is that the Church is conscious of a pastoral responsibility towards all those who belong to the Catholic faith and tries to protect them from situations with which they are unable, or are not yet able, to cope. Any father or mother will do the same. You will object that the Church uses these laws to bind grown-ups. Now, the psychotherapist will know better than anyone else that to be grown-up is by no means the same thing as to be morally responsible. It would be an illusion to assume that all human beings are sufficiently gifted or knowledgeable to be able to see through all the distortions and falsifications of the truth, which are often astonishingly ingenious and refined, or to form competent judgments and arrive at ethically mature decisions at all times and in all places. Unfortunately the formal democracy of our age, living as it does on the heritage of Rousseau's optimism, lulls itself with this illusion, and it will finish up sooner or later in absurdity. At present, with a happy inconsistency, it withholds from its citizens the free disposal of material poisons at least, such as drugs, although it is part and parcel of this illusion that these very citizens are sufficiently intelligent and conscientious to be able to protect themselves from harm. The Church—by which I mean not just some authority in Rome but the New Testament people of God—firmly maintains that there are such things as an absolute truth and eternal moral standards rooted in human nature. Hence the people who belong to this Church, and are aware of their unity in the one faith, will allow their divinely instituted authority every right to pass laws restricting the freedom of the individual wherever it seems likely that the majority are unable to make proper use of their freedom. Whether the individual observes these requirements of the Church or not will remain his own free decision, and there must be no question of violating this freedom by compulsory measures, as unfortunately happened in the past with the Inquisition and its use of the "secular arm".

M.: All the same, it will have to be asked whether these methods of safeguarding the salvation of the individual really produce the desired results. Since we can never know with certainty who has attained his eternal salvation we shall have once more to ask whether those who follow the Church's pastoral admonitions are morally better than those who choose to ignore them.

There is no other method of testing the efficacy of such regulations. Moreover, to judge from the questions you put to me earlier, I assume you would accept that moral behaviour has a certain relevance for the theologian because it enables him to determine what is sin and what is not. Thus, if he wants to find out whether his method of safeguarding salvation is effective or not he will have to find the answer by empirical means. From my own experience, based on psychotherapeutic practice, I do not get the impression that these measures have any visible success as regards individual moral maturity. Grown-up people who take their salvation independently into their own hands, and are not always anxiously asking at every turn what they ought or ought not to do, seem to me, indeed, to be less in danger than the others. There is a good reason for this, and it has to do with the formation of conscience.

E.: As I remarked before, the Church's present legislation stands in need of revision. We shall have to distinguish between the Church's right and the question as to whether this right is exercised with an eye to modern reality. The legislation concerning books originated in an age when there were still clearly defined Catholic regions with a population lacking adequate theological instruction. I am thinking of the turmoils of the Reformation era and the gigantic defensive battle conducted in modern times by the Church against the emancipation of secular culture, a movement which in itself was perfectly legitimate but which went much too far. The Church tried to protect its members by erecting a great hot-house of pastoral rules and regulations round closed Catholic areas. A look at the culture of the West shows that it failed to produce really successful results.

The situation is now very different: the faith has dwindled away among the broad masses of the people, and we are living in a pluralist society. There would be no sense in trying to shelter the faithful Catholic against each and every anti-Christian influence by means of external regulations. Admittedly, a number of individual measures can still be justified, especially since the knowledge some people have of their faith leaves a good deal to be desired. But great care will have to be taken in deciding whether partial measures of this sort, however reasonable in themselves, will be beneficial or harmful in actual practice; they will certainly be harmful if they push nominal Catholics farther from the life of the Church than ever before and at the same time only make it harder for faithful Christians to come to grips with the world around them. After all, this is where they have to live; and their business there is not just to keep their faith intact but to win others by the quality of their lives.

Various specific commands and prohibitions will remain inevitable. But the Church must remember that, as Laotse said, "the more laws there are, the more thieves there will be"; and if the regulations are too specific and their requirements too rigid and casuistical, they will quickly become obsolete and unrealistic.

In 1923, for instance, the German bishops insisted that the sleeves on women's and girls' dresses should reach below the elbow, a requirement which brings a benevolent smile to the face of even the staunchest Catholic today. The accepted threshold of decency has been raised a good way since then, and a number of things which a generation ago would still have offended against modesty are now considered perfectly normal. This does not mean, of course, that a halt will not have to be called somewhere.

Karl Rahner once said that there should be not only principles but also imperatives, an expression which has since become famous. By this he meant that the Christian should not remain in the rarefied atmosphere of abstract general principles but should integrate these principles into real situations by the forming of personal decisions. These imperatives should generally not be formulated by the Church; the individual Christian must provide them for himself, using his knowledge of the situation and his mature sense of responsibility. But all this means that it will be vitally necessary to direct all our attention to the formation of a right conscience and to the education of Christians to adult responsibility.

5. Developed and undeveloped conscience

M.: It is impossible to go into detail here about the development of conscience, but I should like, with all due brevity, to try and outline at least two forms of conscience which differ from one another fundamentally. Between these two extremes any number of different shadings are to be found.

In the one case a person succeeds in forming an independent conscience. The precepts and values he has learnt from others he is able to "incorporate" as part of his own personal attitude; and all the norms by which he acts are internalized in terms of the Ego. But in the other case this does not occur. Here the person remains morally "under age". For him, conscience is a foreign body, and its demands are something external to the Ego and often in opposition to it. It is by no means necessary that he should experience conscience as a foreign body, because he will have been very familar from early childhood onwards with the so-called "dictates of conscience". All he has ever heard is what others require him to do. But people like this are not familiar with conscience as something voluntary and deliberate proceeding from within.

An outsider will be sensitive to the different ways these two forms of conscience work out in practice. Where the conscience has been internalized he will form the impression that the person's moral and religious life comes straight from the heart and has its roots in a harmonized personality. Such a person's relationships with his fellow-men are not blocked by regulations, laws and externalized principles. But it is very different with people whose consciences are externalized and authoritarian. Their moral behaviour is cold and forced, a matter of principle with no warmth of feeling, or at best a matter of unthinking routine. Their morality is performed rather than lived; the acts are there, but the intention is somehow lacking. In psychotherapy it is impossible at first to "get at" people with consciences like these. The moment one starts to question the underlying motives revealed in dreams and fantasies, they try to suppress them by further asceticism and an increase of "practices". The analyst, like any outsider for that matter, constantly receives proof that the suspicions entertained by those with a rootless, non-personal morality are utterly unfounded. Since these people ultimately do not do what they themselves want, but what others expect of them, they need like-minded people to prop up their consciences for them. People of this type set the spiritual tone in many Christian associations—and not just among the sectarians.

It is easy to see the snags of this form of conscience-training. If personal conviction is lacking, it means that these people are unconsciously protesting against the dictates of conscience which they have been expected to make their own; and this revolt, in turn, has to be held in check by an excess of moral acts. The values which the precepts are designed to safeguard are never integrated as the result of a deliberate, voluntary choice. These people have only the most superficial idea of what justice, love, humility or chastity are really about. All they can do is refer to definite acts or forms of behaviour, because they are incapable of sensing the underlying values and leading their lives in accordance with them. Morality of this sort can be described as "morality without conscience", because it very largely lacks the personal conviction which distinguishes genuine conscience. Belief is replaced by an ideology which ensures that faith is measured by external profession rather than by the degree of internalization.

My own impression is that all these characteristics of average religious faith have a great deal to do with the lack of conscience and belief in so much of Christian behaviour. If, as is so often complained, modern man has turned away from the Church, a decisive reason may possibly be found here. It is obvious that only a particular type of person will be ready to embrace an ideology together with all the consequences I have just described. The rest find themselves forced to exist outside the Church and to form their own conscientious convictions for themselves.

Now, if such distorted forms of conscience have become so widespread and have occasionally even been extolled as exemplary, would you agree that it is due, at least partly, to the way in which the Church has exercised its pastoral responsibility? People who understand faith and morality in this way quite often receive the greatest praise and encouragement from bishops and priests. My own view is that the Church could afford to resort much less to measures such as putting books on the Index if it concentrated its educational and instructional measures on internalizing faith and conscience.

E.: It is possible, of course, that our religious instruction is partly to blame for the defective development of conscience among Catholics. This will doubtless occur in any setting where obedience and respect for authority are exclusively promoted or are given undue prominence within a given set of values; or, again, wherever too little trouble is taken to communicate the truths and values on which the edicts of authority are based. It is evidently reprehensible, though only humanly to be expected, that undiscerning, complacent or overweening superiors are more inclined to reward people who obey them blindly than the more independent assistants or subordinates who act according to their own consciences. This applies just as much to the Church as it does to the state or to any business concern.

All the same, I do not believe that the modern world has turned away from the Church primarily because people feel they would be forced to accept a faith and a set of values which have become ideologized and hence spurious. The main impulses came from "outside", though a serious part may have been played at various times by inadequate instructional methods or other instances of the way the Church has exercised its office. Conditions in the Church during the late Middle Ages or the inadequacies in Papal territories in the nineteenth century could be adduced as examples.

But I do not want to use this discussion in order to act as defence counsel for the Church any more than you are concerned to appear in the role of counsel for the prosecution. What interests us both is the task of educating people to act with a mature conscience. And what you have said about these two forms of conscience is of the greatest importance for pastoral work. Moral theologians must not remain content merely with providing a system of ethical norms; they must also realize their responsibility to help Christians towards personal fulfilment. If, in other words, the moral norms they preach are to be actualized in real life, they will have two major tasks to carry out. First, they must not be satisfied with giving people a merely theoretical knowledge of ethically significant values; they must help them to realize these in their lives and try to show that all laws are related to these values. And secondly, they must make sure that this appreciation of values develops into an ability to make conscientious choices—which means effecting a transition from Freud's Super-Ego to the personal integration of ethical norms.

We would be sinning against the New Testament message of the liberty of the children of God if we did not trouble ourselves about the growth of adult responsibility among Christians. Nowadays we are obliged to keep our Christian lives intact in the midst of a pluralist society, and it may well be that we realize this obligation more clearly than in past ages, when the onslaught of dangerous contemporary influences forced the Church to preserve the traditional and to concentrate on pastoral defence-measures. The priorities of a beleaguered city did not leave much room for the development of personal initiative. But it is never easy in any age to educate people to adult responsibility or to govern mature, self-reliant people. Pastors have at all times been faced with human tragedies, and their very sense of responsibility can easily make them anxious; there is then the danger that they will tend to keep their charges in a state of dependence in order to protect them better. No one has described this danger more vividly than Dostoievsky in his legend of the Grand Inquisitor.

M. : But here again, it is not theological theory which provides work for the psychotherapist, but pastoral practice. For example, when one studies pastoral letters and encyclicals from the viewpoint of the formation of conscience one comes across the same thing time and again. Whenever they say that the Catholic has to come to a conscientious decision—say, in pastoral letters before elections—the correct choice is always implied. Anything to the contrary is declared unconscientious. In my study of pastoral letters and encyclicals, I have only very occasionally—and then not until recently—found a few cautious attempts to avoid anticipating the material decision and to offer genuine scope for the exercise of conscience. Yet this scope, too, is diminished by the fact that contrary decisions are obviously not being given a wholehearted blessing.

Even if the Church frequently sees itself as Mother of the faithful and receives respect and honour on that account, it does not mean that it is always right about questions which have not been officially declared to come within the sole competence of the magisterium, nor that its suggestions are always good ones. "Mother Church" can make mistakes, and she can bring up her children badly—it is easy to find evidence of this right up to the present day. Theologians admit this in theory, and you yourself have said so often enough. The theologians speak of the Church's sinfulness, or even of the need for constant reform. But in practice—when advice is being given to the faithful—this aspect recedes considerably. Past mistakes are covered up with hasty explanations, and present abuses are admitted only with the greatest reluctance. There are, it is true, signs that the Church is making more cautious use of its authority; some practical conclusions are evidently being drawn from this theoretical admission of fallibility.

E. : In that case, perhaps, moral theology and pastoral practice are not quite so remote from one another; it is only human that there will be a time-lag before newly gained knowledge bears fruit in everyday life.

M. : All the same, it should not be forgotten that the decisive factor in the individual Christian's life is pastoral practice and not "expert discussion". The expert will know that the existing solution to a problem is not the best possible, and certainly not the last word. But this is not the attitude of the faithful, who will go on taking what is offered to them as revealed, unchanging truth so long as it is formulated in concrete terms for specific situations. They will try to model their life and salvation around it. Thus whenever sermons, instructions or pastoral practice fail, it is always the faithful who suffer. I am thinking here, for instance, of people who try to base their lives on what their priest tells them and then, in later life, discover that they have been taking his words too literally. I have met quite a lot of people whose bitterness has caused them not only to turn their backs on the Church but also to warn their children against making a mess of their lives in the same way.

In the Church—as, for that matter, in political life or in the scientific world—there is a culpable sloth which can most certainly not be explained away in terms of an inevitable time-lag. And the faithful who are not trained to moral responsibility have to suffer the consequences.

For this reason it seems to me important to take a closer look at the effective idea many of the faithful have of the Church as Mother of the faithful, since images like this are often to blame for a number of abuses, as well as for the consequences I have just described.

6. The Church as Mother of the faithful

M. : To start this off on the right lines I should like to mention our changed attitudes towards parental authority, a phenomenon which is based, to a certain extent at least, on the findings of psychoanalysis.

Times were when the parental word was accepted unthinkingly and unconditionally, and when parental authority was final even when it was wrong—and these times are still not completely ended in a number of countries. During the last century this uncritical recognition of parental authority was also strongly emphasized in ecclesiastical quarters; one need only take a look at the Examinations of Conscience printed at the time.

In our own day the authority of parents is looked at more critically. A mother—and this is the example which interests me here—is not a good mother just because she cares for her child, rears it and makes great sacrifices for it. In the same way a father is not a good father just because he goes to work for the family. The subjective attitude is now stressed much more strongly than it was in periods when external circumstances—which were often very difficult indeed—caused parents to be judged mainly by the external provision they made for their children. In our modern civilization sickness and want have been very largely reduced, and this has enabled people to look more closely at parents' subjective attitudes. Thus, a mother who does everything for her child may be a harmful mother; not because of what she does, but because her underlying attitude may be a threat to the child's development. Comparisons with Holy Mother Church will now generally tend to remind people of the sort of mother who sacrifices herself in order to reduce her children to a state of dependence, which prevents them from growing in self-reliance. Mothers like this are generally quite unaware of any such motives and think they are doing everything for the good of their children. But the children feel the consequences of such attitudes all the more. Serious crises can develop, especially in the phase of transition to adulthood, and the child has to pay the price for his mother's attitude in the form of psychic disturbances and even a broken spirit.

Would you agree that this state of affairs—which psychotherapists come across day by day—might make it easier to understand a good many analogous things which go on in the Church? The Church wishes to be respected as a self-sacrificing mother, but it fails to notice that its sacrifices are motivated by a desire for the children's dependence rather than for their welfare. In this way it is blocking something which is absolutely necessary for free, personal moral development—the training of self-reliant consciences.

E.: I think this will have to be admitted. One should not forget that the images used to describe the Church (though not the dogmatic pronouncements) have undergone considerable transformations over the centuries. While early Christianity saw the Church primarily as the new people of God and the body of Christ, the Middle Ages put the major emphasis on priest and office. During the era of absolutism and its idea that subjects had only a limited understanding, the authority of the Church could hardly help feeling itself to be the guardian of a scarcely adult flock. Here is not the place to trace and account for this development, but the picture of Mother Church has not been without its advantages. It has at least ensured that its official authority has kept a warmer and more personal touch. Nonetheless, it does give rise to the danger you have mentioned.

The most recent development in Church thinking on this matter is more in line with early Christianity, but this certainly does not mean that the present Council has forgotten the maternal aspect of the Church. This aspect was familiar even to the early Christians, though with a distinctive difference in emphasis; the supernatural fecundity of Mother Church rather than anxious pedagogy. Nowadays the image of the new people of God has come to the fore, and the consequence is that the Church can no longer be considered as a purely sacerdotal Church, even though there can be no question of abandoning the ecclesiastical authority which derives straight from Christ. The Church is made up of priests *and* priestly people. One could put this another way by saying that the dialogue between authority and people is essential to the Church. It was not for nothing that Pius XII himself spoke of the need for public opinion in the Church, and in doing so he approved of this dialogue. Hence the ancient mystical idea of the Church as the supernaturally fruitful mother will now come to be complemented by the idea of the "modern" mother who, while retaining all her authority, is a friend in whom her children, both grown-up and still growing, can confide. The world is becoming more democratic, and the more this image of the Church becomes established the less danger there will be that maternal fussiness will cause neuroses or stand in the way of growing self-reliance in matters of conscience. But the Church is also of this world, and all vital processes require time and patience.

7. The integration of the sexual

M. : When, at the beginning of the century, Freud wrote his essay *Unbehagen an der Kultur* he spoke straight to the heart of many of his contemporaries. The repression of sexual drives referred to by Freud appeared to many to be an excessively high price to pay for a little bit of culture.

We now know, of course, that Freud's general formula "culture equals repression" is not the last word about culture. But we also know that he was perfectly right in his critique about essential aspects of contemporary sexual morality. The acuteness of his analysis laid bare all its dishonesty, prudery and hypocrisy. The sexual morality of the Churches played its own part in this "unbehagliche Kultur". One has but to read the manuals of moral theology to see how far Church-dictated conscience helped to distort sexuality. Whatever the socio-

F

logical, historical and psychological causes of this twisted attitude may have been, the Church certainly legitimized it both in its pastoral work and in the confessional. Despite the healthy outlook of many theologians, both forerunners and contemporaries (August Adam, for example, in his book *The Primacy of Love*), the Church never succeeded in preaching a sexual morality more in keeping with the order of creation, and thus failed to call a halt to all the anxiety, prudery and dishonesty.

As has so often happened with spiritual developments, the more genuine and realistic view had to assert itself outside the Church, and even in opposition to the Church. The share of psychoanalysis here should not be underestimated, particularly its assertions about the significance of childhood for mature sexuality, which must now be taken as scientifically established.

As a result, the face of moral theology is very different from what it was half a century ago, and attempts are being made to overcome the dualism of instinct and spirit, pleasure and reason, and the animal and the human. It is now usual to refer to the personal element in sexuality, and emphasis is placed on the human possibilities it opens up; pleasure is no longer roundly denigrated as an evil which unfortunately cannot be avoided. In their instructions to engaged couples, as well as in sermons and in the confessional, many priests are trying to put the new theological theory into practice.

Do you feel that these efforts have had any practical results as regards healthy sexual life among believing Catholics? I am asking this because it seems to me that many of the faithful are not able to understand the theological concepts at all, or, what is more important, to incorporate them into their personal lives in such a way that their sexuality becomes "personally integrated".

E. : I am convinced that this healthy development in regard to sexuality and the body will be successful, and perhaps for the very reason that the sex-drenched atmosphere of the modern world is, in effect, a devaluation of the personal and human aspects of sexuality. Indications of this have come even from medical quarters.

As far as religious and moral practice goes, not merely among Catholics but among Christians as a whole, it must be borne in mind that the older people remain very much influenced by what was impressed upon them in childhood. Thus, although they take in many modern ideas at the intellectual level, they are no longer able to assimilate them fully into their own experience. This is also true of many priests who are by no means reactionary; they may be open intellectually to all the authenticated findings of the secular sciences but remain unable any longer to remould their personal lives accordingly. Hence the way they expound these findings may lack the "infectious" character of first-hand personal witness. This is a very important task for the future training of priests—a point we have already touched on.

M. : It is not at all seldom for psychotherapists to find that individual Christians, despite the best of intentions and the greatest openness of mind, do not profit sufficiently from the changes in theological interpretation. For example, we quite often come across women with a strict Catholic education who were never capable of orgasm and have never become so. These women do not think of their symptom as something extraordinary or unnatural. In fact, they think it is perfectly natural to accept intercourse as a more or less unpleasant duty, to be performed as a favour to their husbands or even out of love of Christ.

Another instance might be the cases where married people refrain from marital intercourse before receiving the sacraments or going to church because of a more or less conscious feeling of guilt they have concerning the sexual act.

I am referring to these things simply because education to

healthy sexuality as a vital physical experience is governed only to a certain extent by new theological interpretations. What generations of Christian families have turned into a tabu cannot all of a sudden be experienced in a natural and personal way. Furthermore, sexual development depends so much on individual development in childhood that the burden of education cannot be placed upon the shoulders of the theologians alone. Theological influence will be more effective if it is aimed at the children indirectly *via* the parents rather than directly at people whose sexual lives are already hard-set.

Nonetheless, it is still worth mentioning some peculiarities in the way moral doctrines are presented, because they have a disturbing influence on mature sexual development.

a) Inhibitions caused by an externalized concept of sin

M. : It is quite common to find among Catholic Christians a concept of sin which is governed more by the letter of the law than by conscience. Now, it seems to me that externalized concepts of sin and guilt are, at least partly, a product of pastoral preaching and instruction. We brought out this point when we discussed Pius XII's misgivings about the methods of free association.

If the attitudes underlying misgivings of this sort are transferred to the development of human personality, particularly in the sexual sphere, it will be much easier to appreciate the inhibitions caused by this concept of sin. Mature sexuality—or, as moral theologians would say, personally integrated sexuality—must come from within and have its roots in the depths of personality. But if this is to happen it is vitally necessary that all desires and inclinations, such as the sexual or aggressive drives during childhood and adolescence, should be given a chance to become accepted by the Ego and to be incorporated into the Ego. This process is different for each person, depending on disposition, environment and early childhood development. And occasionally a person will simply have to go through certain phases which a moral theologian would designate as sinful, but which a psychologist would see as necessary steps on the way to development. But it is impossible to lay down any universally valid casuistical rules for individual variations of this sort. Attempts have been made to do this—as can be seen from some Examinations of Conscience. But all they have succeeded in doing is to confront many people with two alternatives: either to suppress their instincts, which is very harmful to personal integrity, or to live them out unrestrainedly and to the full. In neither case will sexual integration be achieved.

E. : We would both reject any concept of sin which takes no account of the underlying intentions and simply enumerates individual acts. But I think further clarification will be needed here, for otherwise ethical misgivings may lead the pastoral theologian to ignore a very important finding of depth-psychology. You say, for example, that sexual and aggressive drives must be accepted by the Ego and that a person will have to go through certain phases which the moral theologian considers sinful but which the psychologist treats as necessary steps on the way to development.

It might be possible to explain the situation as follows. A young person must learn first of all simply to accept as a fact all confusing new forms of experience, such as the awakening of sexual desires during puberty. A priest who is on the alert about these things will take care that no anxious repression results; he will attempt first of all to explain what the new experiences are all about, and then to point out the values behind them and the significance they will have in later life. Not until last will he talk about the dangers.

But there can be no question of the means to this end

taking the form of a free and fully deliberate gratification of such urges outside their rightful context, especially since this would only obscure their personal significance. A young person will become aware of pleasurable possibilities as soon as he feels the surges of sexual desire. He should be told that this pleasure is good if experienced within the context of meaningful sexuality; at the same time he should also struggle to resist the urge to induce sexual pleasure at will, though the struggle should be motivated by his awareness that personal values are at issue and should not cause him to get worked up or anxious. Freud's "bell-glass of denial" is a valid educative principle even outside the field of neurosis-therapy.

The priest must have the courage to take upon himself the risk attendant upon any attempt to encourage young people to learn the meaning of sexuality through a positive acceptance of its stirrings—and the risk, of course, is that their control over their newly-felt impulses may not always keep pace with what they realize at the level of the mind. The more he feels his responsibility the more he will be tempted to teach young people to repress their urges. But this only makes everything worse. Without exposure to temptations, free, responsible decisions will never be possible. For this reason he must always remain ready to help and encourage young people whenever they are being assailed by temptations.

b) *The masking of ethical reality*

M. : There is, it seems to me, another aspect of this external concept of sin which can hinder the development of mature morality and the integration of drives within the Ego, and this is the way the *materia* of sin is interpreted. Sin is defined by the theologians as a turning-away from God, and this is the way it also exists in the minds of many of the faithful. In more mitigated forms one will speak of offences against God or acts of defiance towards the Divine Majesty or opposition to Christ. But this definition of sin does not correspond to the real ethical situation. To put it more precisely, it obscures and distorts real experience. One person may speak ill of his neighbour and wish him ill, another may be inordinately vain and self-satisfied, and another may be a coward; but it cannot be said that these people are deliberately turning away from God or trying to offend him. Reflection on God in such cases is fragmentary and unspontaneous. The reality at issue is the neighbour's ambition, or the profound insecurity which leads compulsively to vanity, or the fear of pain and persecution which makes a person a coward. The more the real facts of the case are lost to view, and the more they are cloaked beneath a global concept of sin as opposition to God, the more remote people become from the genuinely ethical. It will become increasingly impossible for them to adopt any ethical attitude towards themselves and the world around them, or to relate their actions to any ethical values.

For this reason we often observe that Catholic patients are completely unable to recognize their vices for what they actually are, such as hard-heartedness, vanity, self-satisfaction and so on. They are also incapable of saying why such and such a form of behaviour should be so bad. They immediately come out with the comprehensive explanation that it is a separation from God. This concept of sin is a phenomenological disruption produced by unspontaneous reflection; and it smothers all sense of values. And it is probably one of the reasons for externalized Christianity and for the deficient sense of values among Christians such as I have already outlined. A conventional or an ideological Christian has no feeling for the genuine content of his sin. Since he is constantly directing his gaze upwards he becomes quite incapable of seeing the reality before his very eyes.

I do not think that my interpretation here is all that far from the New Testament. In the passage where the Last Judgment was described those who had been saved or condemned pointed out that they had not seen Christ and for that reason could be neither condemned nor rewarded. Christ took the phenomenological reality seriously and did not try to justify his judgment by appealing to things which lay beyond people's experience. He said quite baldly and bluntly: you have widows, prisoners and the poor. That is sufficient to show whether the real situation has proved you guilty or brought you eternal salvation. But he did not say that they ought to transcend the reality of experience and consciously reflect on Christ in their actions.

Let us now apply this principle to the development of sexuality. Such Christians cannot experience even their sins against the sixth commandment for what they really are any more than they can achieve the personal integration of their desires. They grope around in the dark with their catalogues of virtues and vices, commit the same sins over and over again and receive absolution, but are never able to achieve any real sense of what sexual love is about. Theologians know this well enough. But in many cases their knowledge fails to become effectively embodied in preaching and instruction.

I should like, therefore, to ask you how modern theology sees the relationship between the faith of immediate conviction and the faith of mere reflection. In what way do you think the believing Christian should draw God into his concept of sin?

E.: If the principal Christian commandment consists in the love of God and one's neighbour then sin must always comprise a loveless attitude towards God—which, after all, is its ultimate essence. But this should not be short-circuited in the way you have occasionally encountered among your Catholic patients. Ever since Augustine Catholic moral teaching has defined sin as *aversio a Deo et conversio (inordinata) ad creaturam*. Thus both aspects of sin should be kept in mind; to turn lovelessly away from God means to turn inordinately to something created and temporal which appears to the sinner as desirable, or at least as potentially pleasurable.

To see what the proper view of sin should be it might be well to compare it first with morally good Christian behaviour. If someone gives something to another and does so only for God's sake, in other words, directs his gaze away from the recipient, then he is acting in an un-Christian way. You were quite right in referring to Christ's account of the Judgment (*Matt.* 25:31 ff.). Behaviour is morally good in the Christian sense when a person in need of help is regarded directly and seen as deserving of love in his own right. The specifically Christian element comes in when the particular created value to which response is being made—in this case a fellow-man—is seen in relation to God and allows the love of God or of Christ to shine directly through it. But it is by no means necessary to be expressly aware of this in every individual act. It is enough to look at the immediate temporal motive, though in the case of genuine piety there will always be an echo of the dialogue with God at a deeper level. But this is not true the other way round. If something is done for love of God alone without any consideration of the temporal value of the action, insofar as this is done with full consciousness then the action will be of questionable moral value. Such behaviour is ultimately featureless, and can very easily become spurious.

Now if we take a look at sin, it is obviously possible that someone may refrain from an action simply because God has forbidden it: because it is an offence, say, against the eighth commandment. Admittedly there may well be situations where this is the only factor which remains psychologically effective, because judgment as to the objective wrongness of such an action may easily be ousted by physical desire. But this is not a normal condition; if an intensely personal action is done or left undone "for love of God alone", it will lead ultimately to a practical legalism. If a person remains consistently truthful even though a lie holds out the prospect of advantage, his behaviour should be governed by the immediate conviction that truth and truthfulness are worthwhile in themselves and that it is odious to lie.

Although the essence of sin consists in turning one's back on God and his love, it is not necessary that there should be any express awareness that an offence, say, against the truth also involves an offence against the order of creation laid down by God who is himself Eternal Truth. Nonetheless, if a person is really religious, his judgment as to the unworthiness of his behaviour would hardly be without some thought of God.

What you have said on this point is perfectly right, and when it comes to warning people against sin a priest or teacher should not make things easier for himself by appealing simply to the love of God or by referring merely to divine commandments and impending punishment. He must take the trouble to point out the intrinsic falseness and worthlessness of all morally objectionable behaviour. For example, he should make it clear that it is one thing to be indignant over the odious behaviour of someone who has done you some definite wrong, and another to hate him; hatred is a false response to the dignity of the person, and a sinner does not completely lose this dignity because of his sin. Your experience as a psychotherapist proves that we shall have to pay much more attention to this in practice. At the same time, Christian values should include the clearest possible sense of the way a single sin can disrupt, and even possibly destroy, the divine dialogue in our lives.

M. : This question has a practical bearing on the phenomenon of repentance. Psychotherapists not infrequently find among Christians an inability to repent properly because there is no personal contact with ethical reality. A routine Christian may repent out of love of God, and yet not see why his transgression is all that wrong in itself. But very often, since his Christian education has not enabled him to grasp the real meaning behind the commandments for himself, the thing he repents of is at best the transgression of some law; the result is a routine, outward repentance with no prospect of amendment.

E. : To this I should say that the only thing which provides an effective motive for religious repentance is a direct realization of the falseness and worthlessness of sinful behaviour, because this is the only way a sinner can come to acknowledge how greatly he has offended against the divine order of creation and redemption and how lovelessly he has behaved towards God, or towards Christ. In this sense, if there is no true Christian insight into what is morally good and what is sinful, then there can be no repentance.

8. Birth-control: personal decision versus external authority

M. : In very recent years the Church has been moving gradually further away from the predominantly biological concept of marriage. Emphasis is no longer being laid exclusively on generation as the primary end of marriage; conjugal partnership is being treated as equal in importance. But theology has gone half of the way and no farther. Conjugal partnership has certain anthropological consequences, and these are not being positively affirmed. The clearest indication of this is the Church's position as regards birth-control.

Continence apart, the Catholic Church rejects any method other than the Ogino-Knaus method. We shall take a look later at its reasons for this rejection. What interests me here is the influence which a command binding under pain of grave sin can have on love in married life. As I see it, this influence is most evident from the fact that one method alone is declared to enjoy divine approval while all the others are declared sinful and unnatural. That this selectiveness is itself "unnatural" has been pointed out often enough in many different quarters. And it is unnatural because the sexual love-relationship is not left to a free decision based on personal development and the particular situation. Instead, it is regulated from outside. The distinctive feature of the rules here is precisely that they are "from outside" and run completely counter to personal needs. Cases where personal needs and external rules coincide with one another are probably exceptional and cannot be held up as an ideal norm. For this reason it must be accepted in principle—and not just as a matter of fact—that any attempt to impose a norm cuts right across the individual sexual rhythm of different married couples.

It also runs counter to the laws governing the development of conscience. As we have already indicated, a conscience which reacts mainly according to external rules laid down by other people can hardly be called a conscience in the proper sense of the word. Such a conscience lacks the internal, personal aspect; but without this there can be no decision as to the way an individual situation is to be brought into harmony with external norms. But the Church itself cannot be interested in a hollow, externalized conscience; unless, of course, it is going to remain content with an externalized Christianity. And for another thing, it preaches the need for married people to integrate "sex, eros and agape"; yet these differ from case to case. Among adults such integration can be reached only to a very limited extent by means of doctrine and verbal instruction. Married people must assume the responsibility and discover it for themselves.

To my mind, the best thing for the moral theologian to do would be to respect this law and refrain from anything which might hinder the personal integration of sexuality. This would achieve much more than all the theoretical admonitions, which are often still expressed in language which means little if anything at all to the average Christian.

Among the influences which help to prevent married couples working out their sex-life responsibly for themselves are the Church's provisions regarding the use of contraceptives. It is well known that the sexual desires of quite a lot of women are at their strongest precisely at the time of ovulation, when, in other words, the chances of conception are extremely high.

Systematic enquiries carried out in other countries, as well as medical experience in general, have shown that married people make use of the contraceptive method which is best in keeping with their particular situation and their conjugal relationships as a whole. And by "best in keeping" I mean one which helps man and wife to work out their marriage in the way most conducive to conjugal love and harmony, with all the advantages this will have both for themselves and for their children. Contraceptives can obviously be used irresponsibly, but if it is possible in principle for them to be used in a morally legitimate way then this constitutes no real objection.

E. : At present it is somewhat difficult for a moral theologian to give any answer, because a lively discussion is going on in the Church among the experts; and according to the papal instruction of 23 June 1964 the Church's position is in the meantime to be taken as still binding. It would be best to leave this discussion aside for the moment and reply to what you have said about the traditional arguments of the magisterium. This will be the best way of bringing out the fundamental ideas of the Church; and these will never change, even though new assessments of natural data may make it necessary to draw different conclusions from them.

You say that the restriction of birth-control to the Ogino-Knaus method is unnatural and constitutes an external law applied to all marriages without any regard to the individual situation. And you say that the imposition of such norms cuts right across the individual rhythm of different married couples not only in fact but also in principle. The magisterium of the Church would deny that the law is "external". Its arguments, indeed, are based on the constitutive elements of human sexuality. Since the conjugal act is intimately bound up with generation, any direct interference with its physiological integrity is contrary to nature, as Pius XI and Pius XII have both stated. But the "safe period" does not interfere with natural integrity. Where a sufficiently grave reason is present, it is permissible for married people to make use of a natural factor, namely the conception-free days. That this method may not correspond to the rhythm of sexual desire—which in any case, according to medical psychology, is highly variable and thus modifiable—indicates that it is only an emergency measure, a lesser evil. But these difficulties cannot be remedied by ignoring the laws of creation.

This argument shows that there is no contradiction to the laws governing the development of conscience. The internal, personal aspect essential to all conscientious decisions is certainly allowed for here, even though the decisive factor is metaphysical rather than psychological; hence people's consciences are not being subjected to any external norm of positive legislation but to a requirement of the natural moral law.

The integration of sex, eros and agape is certainly highly desirable and must be worked out by married people themselves in the way best suited to their particular situation. But this process is tied to the essential structures of marriage, the requirements of which include not only personal elements but also the preservation of biological integrity. It is certainly legitimate to try and secure all the benefits of conjugal love and harmony; but this does not dispense anyone from the obligation to test the moral acceptability of the method used. Where the means are morally indifferent the goodness of the end will bestow a morally positive quality on them. But if they are in any way morally negative then even the best of ends cannot make them morally permissible. This principle must be made clear because the psychotherapist is concerned with a psychic development, and all the individual factors involved here are ultimately seen and assessed in the light of that development. This is perfectly right, but it does not in the least alter the fact that many methods or practices applied at certain points during this development possess in themselves a moral quality which ethically may be either positive or negative. And their moral quality remains constant even when it comes to fitting them into a meaningful and, in itself, morally desirable pattern of life, and it must be taken into account by the individual conscience.

M. : Even Catholic couples are no exception to the trend towards sensible family-planning. The decline in the number of children in Catholic families can be taken as evidence. It would be very easy to ascribe this to moral decadence; but if we are not prepared to do this, we might well see it as a sign that more and more Catholic families are making their own conscientious decisions as to the best way of working out their married lives. Since it is their own individual life and salvation which is at issue, can they—or even should they—wait until the Church has assimilated the findings of modern science about the nature of marriage and repealed what is at present being proclaimed as a divine commandment? In the Catholic population there is a growing conviction that certain ecclesiastical formulations regarding the order of creation, such as the divinely appointed form of government, are to be understood historically and should not be taken as infallible truth.

There is a world-wide trend to up-grade marriage from a community of biological generation and social function to a community of personal love. But the moral theologians are indirectly blocking this development when they declare some contraceptive methods to be permissible and others impermissible, and I should like to know the arguments on which this attitude is based. And there is something else which might be added. The trend towards the community of personal love can be seen from the fact that people today think of a marriage for reasons other than love as something "unnatural", unlike earlier ages, when parental recommendation, dynastic and professional interests or the like were the generally accepted motives.

E. : If families are deciding for themselves the best way of working out their conjugal life and thus moving, even in the sexual sphere, from a conscience guided merely by authority to one based on deeper insight and an active sense of values, then it is very much to be welcomed; what is more, this is the most burning concern of any pastoral theology of marriage. Ever since Pius XII the Church has been giving more and more explicit approval to responsible parenthood and the family-planning it involves. There is always the danger of abuse and moral decadence, but the Church knows that these are not the only factors behind the limitation in the number of children; there are also factors such as the imminent population explosion in the developing countries and the social and cultural changes in the older civilizations.

Family-planning, however, presupposes not only an active conscience but also a properly educated one. For this reason the Church will continue to assert its pastoral teaching authority even with mature and responsible Christians; and there can be no question of this authority being swayed by considerations of whether many or only a few Catholics are following its teachings. Today, it is true, many married people who can most certainly not be accused of any lack of genuine faith or conscientiousness are arriving at decisions which depart from the requirements of the Church; and this must be taken by the Church as a warning that the attitude it has hitherto adopted will have to be thoroughly re-examined.

This re-examination is going on at the moment—which brings me now to your question about the arguments on which the Church bases the permissibility or otherwise of contraceptive methods. Scripture contains nothing on the matter. The Church, therefore, has to resort to the natural moral law, and in virtue of divine revelation it considers it its right and its duty to provide the authentic interpretation of this law. Its task will be to derive the appropriate moral norms from the essential nature of persons and things. The current discussion on marriage shows very clearly that all the detailed problems such as the permissibility of the so-called anti-baby pill can ultimately be solved only if the true nature of marriage is grasped. Extremely important here are the many new findings of the secular sciences—biology, psychology, medicine and sociology—and they have to be considered in any argument based on the nature of marriage. As a result of new findings, theological as well as scientific, the doctrinal pronouncements of the Church have long been showing signs of a tendency to pay more attention to the personal aspect of marriage. The acutely urgent question today is how to fit the biological function of marriage, which till now has been either exclusively or at least excessively emphasized, into our modern idea of marriage as something embracing the whole human person, body and soul together. The question is whether it will ever be permissible, either as the general rule or in case of urgent need, for married people to intervene in the biological process with the aid of rational and responsible measures, or whether the supra-personal purpose of marriage in the service of procreation means that the integrity of the biological sphere must be preserved whatever happens.

Within the present limits we can go no farther into this

problem. As things are at the moment it is still uncertain what decision the Church will come to; perhaps by the time our words are in print we shall see the matter more clearly. One thing is certain, and that is that the Church will never depart from arguments based on the essential nature of marriage; but it is also certain that the principle of responsible parenthood will remain valid. And it should not be forgotten that, however crucially important it may be to come to a moral decision in particular crises and conflicts, the Christian conscience must remember that it is of even greater importance to have a scrupulous care for the integrity of marriage and the family, and hence for a conjugal love which permeates to every "level" of human existence.

9. Generation as a biological act or an expression of love

M. : The Church's arguments are showing signs of a readiness, until now very largely neglected, to respect the capacity for sexual love of both the sexes, not just of the man alone. The sexual function of the woman, especially in Victorian times, was considered to be first and foremost the bearing of children, to the exclusion of any personal love capable of orgasm.

This attitude was not felt to be unnatural, and least of all in institutions which, like the Church, attached special value to the natural law; and this attitude was to a very large extent connected with the attitude towards children. Earlier ages considered the primary task to be bearing children and making material provision for them. But no one saw—or could have been expected to see—how the love-life of the parents could have much more far-reaching effects on a child's development. These effects have only been discovered in the last fifty years. It has been found that the child's development, his subsequent character and thus also his religious and moral education are influenced very decisively by the personal attitude of the parents, and not just by their external behaviour. It has been discovered that the unconscious personal attitude is a very influential factor in a child's development.

As a result, the love-life of the parents has come to receive its full importance. It can, indeed, be said—and it actually has been said—that the woman's enjoyment of physical love is of no importance whatever for the conceiving of children. But this is true only as far as generation is concerned. It is not true as regards the inner harmony of the woman and hence that of the marriage itself, the creative function of which is not centred in the procreative act alone. Parental creation, indeed, is a permanent process of procreation, and the more the parents are personally attached to one another the better it will be for the child. This means, too, that the parents should be fully in tune with one another, and that the sexual enjoyment of each should be dependent on full sexual enjoyment being enjoyed simultaneously by the other. In saying this I am not trying to push forward the view, often falsely ascribed to psychoanalysis, that the woman must be capable of orgasm every time she engages in sexual intercourse. All I am concerned with is the *principle* that she should be capable of it and that it is an important element in any deeply felt personal love.

It seems to me that the Church's concept of marriage leaves this creative function of the parents out of account. The Church puts by far the greater emphasis on the "biological act"—and only on the functional process at that—as the outward sign of a consummated marriage. But the much more difficult and—for the children at least—decisive process of psychic and spiritual procreation is largely ignored. This may be stretching things a bit, but it can be said basically that the Church's concept of marriage treats the generation of the child as the important thing. What becomes of the child is secondary. And when it comes to the point a child should even be grateful for a life which, because of his parents' failure in marriage, is simply a burden for him.

True enough, moral theology does point to the duty of parents to love and bring up their children, but it is concerned mainly with certain external actions and educational measures. It overlooks the internal attitude. But it is precisely this which determines whether particular educational measures are successful or not.

E. : One cannot, of course, say that the Church is concerned merely with the procreation of children. Procreation and education are mentioned in one breath in the Church's doctrinal pronouncements as well as in canon law. The importance the Church has attached to education can be judged from its determination to preserve the Catholic school.

But you are right in saying that the educational activity of the parents is generally looked at too externally and that the indirect factors in the family are not attended to sufficiently. It may well have needed depth-psychology to bring out fully for the first time how important the personal love between the parents can be in this connection. Could you, perhaps, make this more explicit with an example taken from your own experience?

M. : If I were to describe concrete examples I could—and would have to—fill a whole book with them, because each individual case requires an exact analysis of the particular set of circumstances and the resultant effects on the child's personality. All I can do here is refer to the very varied studies which have clearly demonstrated how neurotic and psychotic disturbances can arise. But it might be possible to boil all this down by constructing a model example. Within the limits at our disposal this may help to make clear that even a marriage considered by the Church as exemplary can contain "elements" which will promote neuroses among the children.

We will take a family, praised by priest and parishioners

alike as ideal, where everything appears to be in order, and even more in order than usual. They go to church on Sunday, and even occasionally on weekdays, and family prayers are said together with the four or five children. The bible is read regularly, as well as the books and papers recommended by the Church. They give alms for the poor and needy and are active members of this or that organisation. The father may be on the parish council, the mother in the Mothers' Union. In short, this is a family which does everything which the Church encourages and praises as exemplary. This goes, too, for the sexual sphere where the question of birth-control is concerned. During Lent husband and wife abstain from sexual intercourse for religious reasons.

But if this family is looked at through the eyes of the psychologist rather than those of the Church the marriage may, perhaps, appear less ideal than at first sight. I am not referring here to occasional altercations, nor to the regularly recurring sins which come out in the confessional. I am referring, rather, to a certain remoteness, and hence a certain coldness, between the members of the family. The expressions "distance" and "coldness" stand here for more complicated and differentiated things connected with the general structure of behaviour. This simplification is obviously liable to be misunderstood. For example, anyone looking at this model family could always point out that there is much cheerful laughter, that the mother looks after her husband and children with no thought of self, and that they all enjoy walks and musical evenings together. To talk about remoteness and coldness seems quite uncalled-for, the sort of fevered nonsense which could only occur to psychologists or, better, among depth-psychologists. All the more so since the members of such families are very attached to one another; they can be taken as very good examples of family closeness, the very opposite, indeed, of personal remoteness.

By remoteness and coldness, then, I mean something

different. I mean the remoteness which arises when particular ideological patterns of behaviour are set up as the ideal norm, while all contrary forms of experience are rejected as "something which ought not to be" and tidied away from the picture—though not necessarily from the heart as well. The cause of all this is the parents, who in turn learnt their ideas of marriage in their formative years. They encounter one another primarily in faith, or more precisely, in an ideological modification of their faith. This is where the harmony of their lives together is rooted. They feel they belong to one another mainly because they pray together, go to church, look on marriage as a sacrament, bring up their children in the way approved by the Church, and even because they share a hope in an ideal condition in the next world. Whenever differences of temperament and opinion arise they are suppressed for the sake of "heavenly peace". The less importance the parents attach to their own personal claims the more they will tend to banish them from the marriage as a whole. This can occasionally be seen even at the level of food. What is cooked, and how it is served, is less important than the fact that food is taken prayerfully and in moderation. The same goes for the sexual aspect. I do not wish to become too explicit on this point, but the partners tend to look aside from one another and preserve a certain distance; they never come close together. Things which help bring other couples closer together are turned into something rather contrived and programmatic. They use them to satisfy their own consciences rather than to affirm the individual personality of the other. Closeness can be permitted only up to a certain point.

If married life, including sexuality, is seen from this aspect it may become clearer why even in such "ideal families" everything is not quite so perfect as the Church often assumes. The eldest son, aged eighteen perhaps, is coming to a more and more definite decision to leave the Church as soon as he is grown-up. A somewhat younger daughter, although best girl in her class at school, suffers occasionally from severe depressions. Another child, fourteen let us say, has been afflicted for a long time with incurable eczema. And the eight-year-old son, the youngest, still sucks his thumb when unobserved.

The children's symptoms could obviously take different forms. We are not dealing here with a concrete case but with an abstract family whose conduct in matters of faith receives the approbation of the Church, but whose faith—from the psychological viewpoint—is an ideological distortion. The family, of course, are quite unaware that their faith has been ideologized, for the very reason that their ideological attitude has received praise and encouragement from the ecclesiastical authorities. But the example may serve to show that the inner attitude, unrecognized and perhaps even unrecognizable, can work itself out in ways which could never have been dreamt of half a century ago.

Now, I am not trying to suggest that moral theology should attach less importance to religious life in the family. On the contrary, religion can be a very important factor in holding a family together. But this should not blind anyone to the fact that the sense of Christian values should be sharpened to the point where it is possible for people to discern what may be going on behind an ideological façade. There may be occasions, admittedly rare, when the family could afford to miss Sunday Mass if they see a long-needed opportunity for them all to come together over a long, leisurely breakfast.

All this means, of course, that married people will be making many more decisions for themselves as to the forms of religious behaviour which will or will not help to preserve the family's ties of love and fellowship, as well as its inner religious spirit. Do you, as a moral theologian, consider this admissible? It goes without saying that my remarks will also apply to the regulation of sexual relationships according to personal conscience.

E.: From your abstract example it seems to me not only admissible but even vitally necessary for the father and mother to learn to make their own decisions much more than they have been doing. Above all, the bonds of ideological belief should be dissolved. This couple have been playing a role, as a result, certainly, of unconscious suggestion rather than deliberate decision. But instead of playing out the part of the perfect Catholic family as accepted in current ecclesiastical norms they must encounter one another, consciously and personally, in terms of everyday life and its responsibilities. This will make their life of correct fidelity to the Church seem nothing more than a well-meant "act". In short, this family needs a vital religion governed by God and his Word rather than by outward forms of participation.

This might perhaps make their life together considerably more difficult and problematic at first. But only in this way will there be a chance that the children will not be simply drilled and strait-jacketed. As their appreciation of underlying values grows and their sense of individual responsibility becomes stronger they will have to form personal decisions about norms and practices which have hitherto remained sacred and unquestioned merely because they have never been understood properly.

This task is of central importance and, comparatively speaking, it is of secondary importance to try and decide how much scope can be given to married people to decide for themselves about the forms of religious activity most helpful to healthy, flourishing Christian family life. As far as the requirements of natural moral law or divine revelation are concerned freedom of decision can obviously only touch the ways of putting them into practice. But that, too, is important. For example, it is essentially up to the parents to decide when their child should make his first communion. Within the religious sphere, indeed, there are many things which are not evidently forbidden under pain of sin, and hence there is plenty of scope for wise parental decision—for instance, how much, and what, religious literature they give their children to read, or how far they consider family prayers to be pedagogically advisable, and so on.

As for "Sunday Mass or family breakfast", this will obviously only rarely present any genuine alternative in actual practice; normally there will be no clash, especially if there is a lively, well-founded conviction in the family about the significance of the Sunday celebration of the eucharist for the parish community. In exceptional circumstances one would have to have recourse to the *epikia* we have already discussed. If, as a result of unusual circumstances, breakfast together on a particular Sunday turns out to have such importance for family fellowship that it can be assumed that the Church's legislators would not reasonably impose an obligation to take part in the sacrifice of the Mass, then they should go ahead and continue with their breakfast.

M. : You have spoken of "playing a part" or putting on an "act"; but this could give many people the impression that an ideological attitude can fairly easily be diagnosed as such. But this is not the case. The person concerned will be the last to realize any lack of sincerity. In fact, he will feel so confident about the way he is living his faith that even a priest who has seen through his ideological behaviour will be unable to put him right.

This will become clearer with the help even of a very rough outline of what psychoanalysts mean by ideology. They mean an attitude of mind whereby the actual content of faith—whether it be that of a Christian, an atheist or a Jehovah's Witness—becomes fixed in the mind because of the significance it has for certain intra-psychic processes rather than because of its truth. For instance, a person who considers the enjoyment of meat as evil and harmful in principle will not be avoiding such food because of some objective quality of the meat itself. It is more likely that subjective qualities of the person's own psyche are being ascribed to meat, thus causing him to become a radical vegetarian.

The nature of these intra-psychic processes is of less interest to us here than a number of criteria which distinguish the ideologist from the believer and which can be present in the most varying degrees. Some of them have been brought out in the course of our discussion.

1. The ideologist, unlike the believer, tends not to concentrate his love upon what is near and immediate. Instead, he will prefer to love something further removed in space and time, as can be seen very clearly, for example, in Communist ideologists. But even with ideological attitudes which are not centred round belief in some future utopia there is still a more or less strongly marked inability to show personal love for someone in the immediate vicinity.

2. For the ideologist, principle is more important than reality; where need be, reality will even be ignored or distorted for the sake of a principle. And this does not apply simply to external reality but also to personal honesty with oneself. One's own offences against pure doctrine will be covered up or justified with the aid of ideological catchphrases.

3. The ideologist's conscience, as opposed to the believer's, has a very marked "outward bias". Its goodness or badness is measured by outward actions which can always be demonstrated to other people. Less careful attention, if any at all, is paid to inner motives and attitudes.

4. An ideologist's conscience is more aggressive in character than the believer's. In practice this will show itself in the pitiless condemnation of those who think differently, and it can even go as far as murder in good conscience. One example would be the crimes of the Nazis, though the same can also be said of the cruelties carried out in the name of Christ over the course

of the centuries. In less strongly marked cases an aggressive conscience can be seen as an emotional inability to treat other people as "equal before God". The world is divided into believers and unbelievers, good and bad; one's own group, of course, is particularly close to God.

5. The ideological attitude is a form of inner compulsion and as such it constitutes ultimately an incapacity to achieve a faith based on personal decision; hence a person with an ideological belief will not recognize any "spuriousness", and there is thus a limit to the external influence which can be brought to bear upon him. The positive aspect of the ideological attitude is the considerable immunity from particular morbid symptoms. The symptoms usually appear first in the children, as can be seen from the example I have just given.

One final point seems to me very important when distinguishing between faith and ideology, and so I should like to treat it as a chapter in its own right. It concerns the significance of personal conviction for the communication of beliefs.

10. Authentic witness

M. : In my abstract example I said of the eighteen-year-old eldest son that he was gradually coming to the decision to give up his faith as soon as he left home. I deliberately chose this example because I wanted to point out that the consequences of an ideologized faith can reveal themselves even in the later religious development of the children. In ecclesiastical circles it is often assumed that the educational forms usually called Catholic should definitely have a favourable influence on the growth of faith, but this is obviously not so. A percentage— probably not low—of children with a "Christian education" either leave the Church at a particular time of life or continue to live as Christians in a way which has little to do with real Christianity at all. People often remain in the Church out of habit or because they are afraid of being stigmatized by others; they have never really assimilated what they learnt during their upbringing. This does not mean that those who dissociate themselves even externally from the faith of their childhood have necessarily come to a freer decision about their faith than those who stay put for habit's sake. Ultimately they too, albeit unconsciously, may be dependent on the rigid religious framework of their childhood. The only difference is that their independence takes the shape of a protest. The semblance, at least, of self-reliance has been achieved.

This lapse from childhood faith as a protest against a residual inner dependence on the parents is a widespread phenomenon which deserves rather more attention in ecclesiastical quarters. The Church should start asking itself more seriously whether it is not, perhaps, due to the way the faith is taught that the practical level of faith in many families leaves the children with no alternative but to leave the Church when the time comes. I am thinking here, for instance, of the authoritarian conscience I have already outlined, and the more or less artificial theological principles by which it can be formed. If the conscience, and hence the faith, of the parents is of this sort it will have a more restricting influence on the development of genuine faith in the child than is often assumed, and the reason here is that the personal relations of the parents both to one another and to their children are not adequately accounted for. The New Testament says that good and evil proceed from the heart, from within—a sentence which psychologists would underline three times. No outward form, however well meant, nor even the most carefully observed cult, can smother the influence of the internal reality on the development of the child's personality. It is important even in the family that the faith as preached should correspond to the faith as lived.

E. : Alienation from the Church and the faith as a protest against the parental home is probably a danger which is connected generally with the problem of the generations. It can even happen in a family with a vital faith, particularly when the parents are strong, marked personalities with an unenlightened sense of responsibility, so that they have allowed the children too little scope for assimilating the family religion for themselves. A son or daughter will then quite often choose to protest precisely against the things which are dearest to the parents. This general danger can only be warded off by a watchful, prudent love which educates the children inconspicuously to freedom and allows them just so much freedom as young people can cope with at a given moment.

But what you have in mind is the more complicated case where the parents themselves have no personal relation to their faith but simply ideologize it. I should be inclined to say that things as a rule are rather less sophisticated; it will not be a question of ideology so much as of doing—where religion is concerned—"what everybody else does". As C. G. Jung would say, it is not the Self which is performing the religious acts but the Persona—the thoughtless and uncritical adoption of the current pattern of social behaviour. Such piety is obviously a very grey, insipid affair and for that very reason alone will cause adolescents to yearn for liberation. Moreover, such parents simply do not see how dangerous the dull routine of their religion can be for the religious ideas of their children; their own piety is much too external and unproblematic. At present this cheerless state of affairs is the rule among a considerable number of "still practising" Christians.

Faced with this, the priest will do what Christ himself did, quoting from the Old Testament prophets: remind them that people cannot honour God with their lips when their heart is far from him (*Mark* 7:6). But more than this is done today; one result of theological thinking is beginning to make itself felt in a deepening of the idea of faith, and this may well help to put more life into people's practice. Earlier there were two alternatives: either the Catholic faith, holding tenaciously to a system of revealed truths as set forth by the magisterium, or Lutheran fiduciary faith, meaning simply a personal encounter with the Lord; but these two aspects of faith are now tending to come closer together, to the benefit of both. For the Catholic it is clear that he will continue to hold fast to his belief in the truths proposed by the Church as the deposit of revelation. But today we sense more clearly that this assent must proceed from a personal affirmation of Christ, who, after all, was not simply entrusted with the preaching of individual items of revealed truth but was himself the way, the truth and life (*John* 14:6). And we are now also more clearly aware that we should not go round brandishing our revealed truths like a sort of religious party programme; they have been given to us so that we may "have life, and have it abundantly" (*John* 10:10), and so that our faith may be a living thing motivated by truth. The Church's methods of instruction will be permeated by all this to the extent that theologians and pastors come once again to make fuller use of scripture. You, as a psychotherapist, will obviously see much less of this emerging trend than of the unsatisfactory everyday situation, and you will evidently base your questions on the dangers which arise from it.

M.: But I get the impression that this question still tends to be skimmed over in pastoral practice. It is stated, admittedly, that parents ought also to be an example to their children in the faith. But even where this example is not confined simply to training children to carry out easily teachable forms of behaviour, much too little importance is attached to the way the parents' personal convictions can influence the development of faith in the children. This was the reason why I suggested that, in certain situations, it might have a better effect on faith for a family to decide to prolong its breakfast on

Sunday instead of feeling they absolutely have to go to Church. The Church itself speaks of freedom of faith, but scope must be given for its exercise even where religious forms are concerned. There can be no question that a man will be separating himself from God in the sense of grave sin if, for reasons best known to himself, and hence applying only in his case, he decides not to carry out some religious act. In saying this I am by no means disputing the right and even, perhaps, the duty of the Church to lay down general norms of behaviour; but I do object to the usual claim that obedience to these norms is the best possible way of living one's religion for every person in every situation.

E. : Although I agree with what you say in essence I would be inclined to shift the emphasis a little. It is perfectly true that living faith demands fairly considerable scope in the matter of personal religious practice. Parents do tend to get rather anxious, and it is quite understandable that they should, since we are surrounded by so many signs of cultural and moral decline; all the same, one cannot emphasize strongly enough that they cannot simply transplant their own religious experiences into their children or impress their own style of religion upon them.

The same goes for the "parish" family. I do not mean this so much in the sense that excessive paternalism should be avoided; a parish priest should think of himself as living in the service of his brothers and sisters—though certainly with the additional power and authority of his ordination—rather than as the father of comparatively under-age children. The danger of paternalism has been pointed out by the bishops themselves; with the increasing democratization of the world this danger will become all the more conspicuous.

What I mean is that there has come to be an even more important reason why this vital measure of freedom should be granted for the exercise of personal religious decisions. The liturgical revival in our Church has broken down the old idea of mere "attendance at Mass", or of the Mass as a more or less private "devotion", and replaced it with the idea of the parish celebrating the eucharist together; and the individual Catholic—very much to his own religious advantage—now has his own definite part to play in the community liturgy, though the forms this will take can obviously vary. To the extent that this idea takes over, any sensible priest will do his best to avoid tedium and religious stagnation. For this reason he will respect religious privacy and encourage people to work out their own forms of religious life, since the religious life of the community as a whole can only remain vital and healthy if there is a polarity between the public and the private aspects of religion.

This, moreover, applies not only to liturgical activity but to every aspect of faith—a fact which should be given much more attention.

Time and again throughout its history the Church has found itself obliged to stop theologians smearing each other as heretics; which means that it has had to guarantee the free play of ideas within the bounds of revealed truth and give fair controversy its head. In periods when this pastoral wisdom was ousted by over-anxiety, and attempts were made to impose uniformity on ecclesiastical ideas, estrangement from the Church became much more common as a form of protest, just as in the families we have talked about.

Thus it is an important principle that a certain measure of freedom in matters of faith and piety should be granted, as a life-saving counterpart of the religious life in community— whether at the level of the family, the parish or the Church as a whole. It will then be a secondary question how far it is possible and permissible for the performance of obligatory religious activities to be omitted if a particular situation suggests that some other religious value could best be furthered in this way. Here, again, it is a matter of *epikia*. Many individual commands or prohibitions have come to enjoy a sacred inviolability far beyond their original meaning and importance; and it is precisely when it comes to these that people should use their discretion and act against the letter of the law when there appear to be specially good reasons for doing so. I would say that it is educationally of great importance, and priests should educate people accordingly.

M. : When I started talking about the importance of parents' faith for the development of their children I was trying to show that the inner attitude of the parents is no less decisive than the intellectual enunciation of truths and norms. You then said that this can also be seen in the relationship of priest and parishioners, because there is a parallel here with the parent-child relationship. What concerns me here is not so much the problem of the paternalist priest, which is a perfectly natural phenomenon, since the average Catholic transfers the idea of parental authority to the priest, and from him to a whole hierarchy culminating in the pope at the top. What really concerns me is the complex problem of the credibility and authenticity of witness among priests. Whether the truths of faith are accepted as true or not depends, unconsciously rather than consciously, on the witness himself and not merely on the intellectual content of what he preaches. This point seems to me to have a certain theological relevance, and it is this I should like to refer to now, even if only briefly and in layman's terms.

The Christian faith is, strictly speaking, a belief in a testimony. Hence it is not a matter of holding the truth of certain maxims set down in writing by Christ. The New Testament is, rather, the concretization of what the actual witnesses experienced directly, or heard of from others, as being the teaching of Christ. The message proclaimed by the immediate witnesses included a number of things which even

G

their contemporaries would have considered "incredible"; the outstanding example is the resurrection. For the Christian the resurrection is the very centre of faith, as Paul said: "If Christ has not been raised, then our preaching is in vain and your faith is in vain" (1 *Cor.* 15:14). But the resurrection has a special place of its own, not only among the articles of faith but even as regards its "documentation". Almost all the other "miracles"—as they would have been understood at that time— were performed before a "non-selected group" of witnesses. Anyone present at the multiplication of the loaves, the raising of the dead or the changing of water into wine became a witness of the action, no matter what his personal attitude to the person of Christ. He could take the event as a miracle, and thus as a sign of Christ's divinity—or leave it, just as he wished.

But with the resurrection, the "greatest of all miracles", it is different. Not all and every witness was allowed in here. Only certain witnesses predestined by God saw the risen Christ. Thus something is missing here which was usually there for the other miracles: the presence of people whose attitude towards Christ was hostile, neutral or sceptical. This absence of outsiders is all the more remarkable since the resurrection was the sort of miracle which would probably have given even those more personally remote something to think about. For this was something which had never happened before: a dead man rising again by his own power.

The question, then, is this: why did God—purely from the theological point of view—choose to do without the most completely convincing demonstration of his divinity before a wide public? Doubts about the resurrection, and hence also about the divinity of Christ, over the course of history would not have been so great if Christ had revealed himself even to non-selected witnesses. As a non-theologian, of course, I do not wish to go into this in too much detail.

E. : The theologian, too, will have to leave this question open.

Christ simply chose to act in this way. It might be possible to make it a bit more comprehensible by referring to the fundamental fact that the Redeemer became man at all in the first place. It would seem characteristic of the way the Lord "emptied himself" that he should have left his message entirely in the hands of his disciples; and that he should not have wanted to make our faith any easier, because he wanted us to put our whole heart and soul into it.

It might, of course, be asked, whether the doubts about Christ's resurrection over the course of history would really have been diminished if non-selected witnesses, too, had seen the Lord. This might itself have given rise to many a question, such as the possibility of mass-suggestion. We might perhaps apply here what Christ said in the parable of Dives and Lazarus: "If they do not hear Moses and the prophets, neither will they be convinced if someone should rise from the dead" (*Luke* 16:31). "Faith comes from what is heard" (*Rom.* 10:17), not from our own perception; there is no getting away from this.

M. : The particular manner in which the resurrection was proclaimed gives rise to another question which seems to me, as a psychologist, to be of some relevance. If the resurrection was vouchsafed only to certain predestined witnesses, then the witnesses of so unusual an event must surely have had a quality which led others to believe their testimony. From what I know of the kerygmatic practices of the Church I gain the impression that it tends to place the onus of unbelief principally on the unbelievers. This has been happening for centuries, as can be seen even from theological and religious writings, and in one sense appeal can be made to a passage in scripture: Christ "upbraided them for their unbelief and hardness of heart, because they had not believed those who saw him after he had risen" (*Mark* 16:14). It very often looks as though the Church were laying claim to divine knowledge of human

motives and upbraiding all unbelievers for unbelief and hardness of heart. There can be hardly any other way of accounting
for the barbarities of the Middle Ages or for many of the
things which are said even today about the refusal of
unbelievers to believe.

But if we are not prepared to accept that hard-heartedness
is the sole cause of refusal then we can find another explanation among the theologians, particularly the Protestants with
their various shades of opinion. Faith, just like election as
witness of the resurrection, is something predestined—a
distinction, a grace. If this is the case, then it becomes difficult
once more to see why the Churches have been so little inclined
to act accordingly. They could have left unbelievers in peace
and enjoyed their possession of election and grace. This reminds
me of my old teacher, Nicolai Hartmann, who wrote me a
letter during the war, saying: "Believers have always claimed
to possess a special organ for the divine. Now, I simply haven't
got one. I don't feel I can say anything about the matter one
way or the other." This seems to me to hit the nail on the
head as far as quite a lot of theological arguments are
concerned.

As a layman in theology, however, I still wonder whether
the theological view of faith simply as a grace, and not also
as a free human decision, is in keeping with the biblical facts.
The behaviour of the privileged witnesses of the resurrection
seems to point in a particular direction. They did not keep
their experience to themselves with the thought that they had
received a particular distinction not intended for others. On
the contrary, they treated it as a call to go and communicate
it to others who had not known Christ at first hand, and, what
is more, in such a way that the resurrection could come to be
accepted as an historical fact and as an event of significance for
all men.

E. : I should like to corroborate what you have said, and in two ways. Although faith appears in scripture as a grace, this does not necessarily mean that human freedom plays no part in bringing it into effect. If that were the case, Christ would not have upbraided unbelievers as he did, and he could not have said "he who does not believe is condemned already" (*John* 3:18). Here, of course, the human mind is confronted with an impenetrable mystery and our discussion can go no farther into it; though the words of Nicolai Hartmann you quoted could do with some further elucidation in this connection.

And again, the New Testament message of faith as a grace must be seen together with the demand made to believers and to the disciples: "Go therefore and make disciples of all nations" (*Matt.* 28:19).

M. : Yet the psychological questions this raises seem to me to play scarcely any role in the Church's kerygma. It has become so much of a habit to see faith primarily as a set of truths to be accepted and to forget that faith cannot be coerced by any argument, however subtle and technically correct. Faith is not a belief in certain intellectual truths but primarily belief in a fellow-man who communicates certain truths—one's parents, for example. Credibility is of decisive importance for any coherent, living faith.

E. : May I interrupt you again? I should like to give our discussion of the psychological aspects the clearest possible theological basis. Technically a theologian would not say that we believe *in* a fellow-man. We may *believe* our fellow-man; but we believe *in* God, *in* Christ, which means that the believer sees in him the real partner in the religious dialogue, and thus the living guarantee for the truths of faith. Hence no man can ever be the ultimately decisive reason for our faith, only God. In practice, however, we do come to our belief in Christ by believing a man—by means, therefore, of human mediation.

Another theological distinction can be drawn here. In a qualified sense we believe the apostles, because they were the authorized witnesses of Christ, whose death concludes the New Testament revelation proper. The magisterium of the Church claims the right to preserve the deposit of faith made known to us by the apostles and to propose it as the object of belief in virtue of its infallible teaching authority. Then the Church's bishops and priests possess an official authority in proclaiming the truths of revelation, though here there is no question any longer of accepting what they say about divine revelation as infallible. Even less so in ordinary human interchanges where the truths of faith are passed on, as from mother or father to child. It is the theologian's business to concern himself with this hierarchic gradation of objective authenticity. You, as a psychologist, will ask what significance the human qualities have.

M. : The question of interest to the psychologist is the credibility of the person who proclaims a truth of faith. Before trying to show this from modern examples I should like to refer to a number of passages in the New Testament in which the problem is clearly brought out. In the main these are passages which tell how the witnesses of the resurrection communicated their experiences to others. The striking thing here is the plainness and simplicity of their announcements, considering the "incredibility" of the event. There are no long discourses, no reasons or proofs, no attempts at detailed explanation. On the contrary the apostles simply state the facts in the presence of their hearers, briefly and succinctly: "This Jesus God raised up, and of that we all are witnesses" (*Acts* 2:32). The only people who can talk so simply and convincingly about a highly extraordinary event are the insane or those who, while making their announcement, do not feel that other people take them to be lunatics when they are telling of their experiences. Now, the apostles were most certainly not taken for lunatics. On the contrary, their preaching was so convincing that their message managed to spread with astonishing rapidity, despite all the resistance of the Jewish and pagan world. The experiences of Paul as set down in *Acts* seem to me very significant in this connection. The acceptance of the faith by so many unbelievers is psychologically unexpected, and it seems to me possible only if the witnesses were psychologically credible. The hearers at the time must have gained the impression that the preachers of the new faith—the central element of which was precisely the resurrection—had really seen and felt the risen Christ for themselves.

As a non-theologian I am not so much concerned with whether my ideas about the dissemination of the faith in the primitive Church are correct or not. I want to use my theological speculation simply as a point of departure for a psychological consideration of the Church's propagation of the faith from one particular aspect. The problem can be put like this: do the preachers of the Christian message make any such impression, so that people accept what they proclaim?

Nietzsche talked about the "unredeemed physiognomy of the redeemed". More important though, I would say, than the consciousness of being redeemed is the encounter with Christ as affirmed by those who spread the faith. One will think first of all here of the persons who try, as it were "professionally", to form their lives by Christ. They pray for an hour or more every day, celebrate the Mass and give themselves more than other people to meditation, quite apart from the many ascetic practices which are supposed to help foster a life modelled on that of Christ. Thus, if there is anywhere a group of people who consciously strive to model their lives on Christ, then it is the priests. They even lay claim to being specially chosen from among men, as the epistle to the Hebrews suggests. But do they affect outsiders in such a way as to make them believe what they have to say about their encounter with Christ? Or to put it another way, have these people been so transformed by their turning to Christ that the outsider is able to believe that their encounter, and the preaching which flows from it, is a reality?

My question to you, then, is this: do you consider the problem I have touched on here to have any relevance for the effectiveness of preaching? Has it any decisive importance as regards the growing ineffectiveness of the Christian message?

E. : But can one speak quite so sweepingly of a growing ineffectiveness of the Christian message? There are many indications that we have now got the worst behind us. The effectiveness of Christian preaching does depend, of course, on personal qualities. Christ could hardly avoid mortgaging his work in this way if he wanted to entrust it to men. We have already remarked that this would be the effect of God's "self-effacement" in the incarnation. What the Lord said about the scribes and Pharisees will obviously apply to the sinful, defective representatives of his Church: "Practise and observe whatever they tell you, but do not what they do" (*Matt.* 23:3). There is no perfectionism even in the religious and moral sphere, and least of all in a religion with the lofty demands of the Sermon on the Mount and with the message of the absolute gratuity of grace, the power of which is made perfect in human weakness (2 *Cor.* 12:9). It is not for nothing that the priest at every celebration of the eucharist has to say his Confiteor before that of the congregation.

M. : But I do not think that this theological self-interpretation is of much assistance in the problem of authentic witness. It may well be that theologians and those already in the fold will content themselves with the reasons you have given. But outsiders and unbelievers will not. A look at primitive Christianity will help to make this clear. If the apostles had accounted for their sinfulness as the Church does today it would have been psychologically highly doubtful whether the message, "we have seen the Lord for ourselves", would have been accepted. And finally, there is also a passage in John's gospel, echoed in *Acts* (2:42 ff.; 4:32 ff.), which seems to me to account for the credibility of the witnesses at that time: "By this all men will know that you are my disciples, if you have love for one another" (*John* 13:35).

E. : It is certainly true that the life of the primitive Christian community, according to *Acts*, was marked by an unusual harmony and love. But then again, the apostles had been closely associated with the life and death of Christ, they had met the risen Christ and experienced the miracle of Pentecost; it is only to be imagined that they should proclaim the Good News impressively and convincingly. But it would be a mistake to idealize primitive Christianity. From the Pauline epistles we learn of various abuses, some quite grievous, as at Corinth; and even more clearly from the letters to the seven churches at the beginning of *Revelation*. And the primitive Christian communities had plenty of indications that the apostles were human; I am thinking of the brush between Paul and Peter in Antioch (*Gal.* 2:11), or the "sharp contention" between Paul and Barnabas (*Acts* 15:39). And the trouble Paul had with his "weaknesses"! But I am not trying to detract from the importance of your question.

M. : There is, in fact, a very serious question here, and the theologian cannot be spared. What picture does the outsider today form of the preachers of Christ's message? Does he get the impression that this preaching is based on a genuine experience of Christ? I think not. What I have heard from my fellow-men, both inside and outside the Church, points in another direction. It all suggests that modern man's inability to believe is due much more to the incredibility of the witness than theologians are prepared to admit.

a) The use of "killer phrases"

M. : When believers and unbelievers come out with arguments on this point priests are much inclined to smother them with the sort of answers known in creativity research as "killer phrases". By these are meant replies which are perfectly correct "in themselves" and hence, to some extent, unassailable. The reason, ultimately, for their employment is not to reach the truth or a better solution but to neutralize all uncomfortable arguments by means of perfectly correct generalizations. Critics of the Church often find themselves up against a whole set of favourite killer phrases. This arsenal of ready-made truths contains items like: "We are all sinners"—"The Church has always taught that"—"The Church is not a Church of martyrs".

The use of killer phrases has had the result that critics who should be taken seriously are less and less willing to engage in any discussion with priests. Furthermore, "unbelievers" who are seriously prepared to listen are only able to put their impressions very inadequately into words. These impressions are mostly subconscious, but they help to form an attitude to the priest which makes it difficult, if not impossible, for them to accept the objective content of the faith.

Some of these impressions boil down to an internal contradiction on the part of the priest between the faith he preaches and the faith he lives, and I should like to try and put them together in a pattern.

In the eyes of the outsider the Church—and by this I mean primarily the priests and the hierarchy—seems to take its life from sources other than the faith. The faith as expressed in words and concepts means a life in Christ, it emphasizes the abundance of sacramental grace and even, in many of its hymns and texts, speaks of a love of God unto death itself; yet the faith which people see from outside reveals other sources from which its ministers draw their inspiration. To put it bluntly, these sources are worldly.

E. : You have here put your finger on the most telling and serious argument against the credibility of the Church's message. Obviously, the priest expects any objections against him to be well grounded, as is only fair. Very often the ideas of outsiders or lapsed Catholics on this point are generalities which have been accepted uncritically on hearsay, often with a highly emotional colouring.

I would ask you also to remember the well-nigh super-human effort it requires of a priest to have to perform his "professional" services on a strict schedule, since these services consist essentially of personal and religious acts. He has to recite the prayers in front of the congregation, administer the sacraments and many other things besides, no matter how he may happen to feel at the time.

Anyone who considers the problem of authenticity with a discerning eye will pass a more cautious judgment. The more disturbing and inexplicable a religious message is, the more the credibility of its witnesses will be put to the test. The apostles themselves experienced this at Pentecost when they were taken at first as drunk (*Acts* 2:13)—the ecstasy of their speech found no sympathetic hearers. Now, it is evident that no earthly preacher of the New Testament message will ever be able to bring his life fully into line with his message. For this reason objections against his credibility can only be taken seriously into account when disappointments as to a priest's personal qualities really have something directly to do with his religious credibility. And this is not always the case. Time and again it happens that someone takes offence at a trifle—some remark or piece of behaviour on the part of a priest which has nothing whatever to do with his religious message—and "leaves the Church". If a person is not prepared to be objective in his criticisms then even the best of priests will be of little help.

All this, however, merely adds seriousness to the question of deficiencies which really do undermine the credibility of preachers of the faith. In this connection I think there is one thing which should be borne in mind. A priest, too, bears the burden of *having* to believe. It is one thing to proclaim what one has personally experienced as a witness to the event of salvation—in other words, to preach the faith in an age when the charismatic early dawn of Christianity simply inundates all that is institutional and humanly inadequate in the witness's own person. But it is another thing to be a priest of a world-wide Church, in which nineteen centuries of history have not only caused the charism to give way to the institution, but have also institutionalized much which was historically conditioned and which therefore both can and should be scrapped. And all this makes faith no easier for a person who is not content to accept uncritically whatever others tell him.

The priest has an even heavier burden to bear here than the layman, because the whole of his vocational activity is meaningful and tolerable only on the basis of the religious step he once decided to take—and the same will apply to things like celibacy which cut deeply into his personal life, or the way he has to keep himself detached in so many respects from "normal" life. A doctor remains a doctor and can go on practising whether he believes or not. But a priest who has lost his faith is a nauseating humbug; the only other choice for him is to "go". To my mind it is this, rather than, say, celibacy, which places the heaviest burden on a spiritually alert priest in an age when the Christian faith is no longer taken everywhere for granted and a Christian is forced to struggle constantly against the current.

M.: The priest's situation as regards his faith is doubtless a special one. But this phenomenon seems to me to have problems for his credibility when he tries to go about things with the aid of "unreligious" methods rather than with the resources of his faith. These "unreligious" methods might include, for instance, the cultivation of a false reverence for priests. A priest can very easily let others revere him as one singled out for a life of special suffering, without remembering that other people, too, have had to hold out, with little hope to cling to, and with their faith constantly assailed by temptations. You have only to think of the many concentration camp victims who had to endure their fate without any religious motivation.

The real spiritual distress of many priests should obviously not be overlooked; but on the other hand, it should not be forgotten that they are to a very large extent free from material cares, in this country anyway. On the whole they live rather better than a lot of other people. A priest, just like an official, receives his salary even if he is no longer carrying out his religious duties satisfactorily. And a parish can do nothing to secure the dismissal of a priest who has absolutely nothing of religious value to offer. Priests might well make their witness more credible if they even occasionally admitted the advantages afforded them by freedom from external cares. Things are appreciably harder for a worker with several children.

E. : You deserve every thanks for coming out with this so plainly. Since a priest's faith must necessarily be exposed to temptations it is only too easy not to meet them in a religious way by means of deep theological reflection, prayer and moral self-control; and the more unconscious this reaction is the more dangerous it can be. There is a failure here to come to terms with personal insecurity, and an attempt is made to cover it up with the aid of illegitimate and inner-worldly means; and although these means will not be used as the ultimate basis of religious authority, they may well be used at least to bolster it up. These are the beginnings of possible clericalism. As the official bearers of the Christian message we must be grateful to depth-psychology whenever it catches us fairly and squarely in any attempt to compensate in this way. It would be a good thing if you could give us a few informative examples of such attempts.

M. : We shall have to distinguish here, I think, between the compensatory attempts of individual priests and those of priests as a group. There are as many different variations of the former as there are human beings. As for priests as a group, I have no systematically established findings at my disposal, so I can make no universally valid assertions. All I can do here is pass on the impression formed by people more or less remote from the centre of the Church who feel there are quite a number of things which detract from the credibility of the Church's message.

b) Traditional marks of prestige

M. : First of all comes something relatively harmless, but it puts a lot of modern people off: the pomp and circumstance of the ecclesiastical hierarchy. Titles, regalia and the traditional system of procedure and clerical advancement take the forms which were customary during the age of feudalism. Obviously, the Church does not need to adapt its external appearance to every change in political and social forms, provided that its fundamental principle, the continuity from Christ and the apostles, is made sufficiently visible. But this cannot be said of an organization whose external features are those of feudal power.

The average Catholic, who is not so likely to see things in their historical perspective, tends to believe that this hierarchical system with all its complex titles and vestments has something to do with the religious substance—accordingly he will think of a prelate as standing somehow nearer to divine revelation than a simple priest. The non-Catholic layman, on the other hand, will only accept the secular aspects, and may even attribute a certain beauty to them; but he will have not the slightest sense of anything divine behind all the trappings. These people smile when someone tells them that a bishop is a successor of the apostles, and that his ecclesiastical appointment really makes him one. Quite often these people are by no means ill-disposed towards the Church. They may even esteem it, though not as a divine institution but simply as a cultural force, or a guardian of morality or tradition. Many of them even say aloud what the others vaguely feel—that it is only for reasons of prestige that a bishop claims to be a successor of the apostles. He doesn't really believe it himself, they say; if he did, he would present himself as an apostle, not as an ecclesiastical prince.

These half-formed impressions, and others like them, can be summed up a little less crudely. The prestige-mentality is very much alive even in the ecclesiastical hierarchy itself. But it is not admitted. There is a tendency to act as though all the symbols of authority which characterize the Church's outward appearance had something to do with clerical organization. But a close look shows that these symbols are of secular origin and every bit as questionable as those in secular society. A person who owns a house, wears a coat with a fur collar and drives a Mercedes often wants to be a cut above others and to make his superiority evident at first sight. This behavioural etiquette is something we have inherited from the animal kingdom; the ethical substance is given very short shrift, if any at all—as the Church well knows. The Church, therefore, does not hesitate to take a stand against worldly ostentation as expressed in the hunt after status-symbols. But it fails to take account of its own tendency in this direction. A bishop who could do his work just as well with a Volkswagen prefers a Mercedes 220 or a B.M.W. The thought that he could perhaps help other people by giving up his status-symbol, and, for the matter of that, enhance the authority of his Christian message, strikes him but rarely. Be that as it may, the manuals of moral theology have much less to say on this point than they do about how far engaged couples may go in sexual matters.

Would you see a moral problem in this adaptation to the world and its externalized etiquette, and particularly as regards our problem of authentic witness?

E. : Most certainly. I think we do tend to underestimate the significance of this question. It is all so familar, and so seemingly unalterable—the hierarchical grades, by far the greater number of which cannot claim to have been instituted by Christ, the corresponding regalia, the rather less colourful but still highly variegated array among the religious orders, and all the rest. Very familiar, too, is the radical criticism of ecclesiastical splendour which has been cropping up from time to time over the centuries. So we try to put up with it all as best we can, be it with humour, resignation, pious anger or even a determined love. All the same, what cannot help alarming any pastor conscious of his responsibilities is the question as to whether there is not really more at stake here: the credibility and spiritual authority of those who show themselves to the modern world in this way.

You speak of this problem as one for moral theology; perhaps better, for pastoral theology. And it is certainly a problem. It needs a lot of thought, and there can be no question of simplifying matters, either by presuming the sanctity of tradition or by dismissing the whole lot as the mumbo-jumbo of witch-doctors. A bishop should present himself as an apostle, not as an ecclesiastical prince, you say. Both of us are agreed in wishing that all traces of ecclesiastical princedom would completely vanish as soon as ever possible. But if a bishop (in his official functions at least) were to turn up in the homely garb of a Galilean fisherman or that of the tentmaker of Tarsus it would be just as prejudicial as any feudal magnificence.

However sober our modern ideas may be, we should not forget that the Church is not dealing with angels or pure intellectuals. The ordinary man expects a momentous spiritual reality to be expressed in a suitably impressive and dignified manner. The temptation to spiritualize all this away has come up time and again in Church history, and those who have succumbed to it have quickly found themselves in barren isolation. To turn for a moment to your handy example, which has often been brought up. Whether it always has to be a Mercedes 220 or a B.M.W. is open to discussion; I myself remember with great pleasure how an amiable Austrian bishop once took me with him in his Volkswagen 1200. But a Volkswagen 1200 would be a bit of an understatement in this country; it is simply impractical for the many visitations of a bishop, who has to take his vestments with him because the normal parish does not keep a set.

But to return from this little banality to fundamental principles. It will remain necessary to bring home the dignity of spiritual and ecclesiastical offices with some measure of impressiveness in a Church which can no longer claim the charismatic charm of the "grain of mustard seed" (*Matt.* 13:31) and is forced to present itself to modern man as a worldwide institution with the marks of a long history upon it.

To what extent the external forms can be retained in view of the problem of credibility is another matter.

M. : And this is precisely the point I am getting at. I have no doubt at all that the external, ostentatious aspect of the Church was felt to be a fitting expression of the Church's clerical hierarchy in feudal times. After all, the people of the Middle Ages built enormous and magnificent cathedrals in the tiniest of towns even though their own living conditions were wretched. They took their sense of security for the most part from the Church, which promised them paradise as a compensation for the sufferings and miseries of that time—and these were not inconsiderable, as compared with today. But modern man no longer looks on the Church in this way. His security comes mainly from science, technology and the state. Consequently the Church has become much less important for him in this sphere, certainly less important than for medieval man, who found the Church as something definite to hold on to in a time when he was threatened by premature death, poverty, infant mortality, plagues, diseases and wars. He knew no alternative to the Church, and would thus have been able more easily to overlook the crass contradiction between external trappings and inner substance. The pressure of external distress forced people to seek the Church's abiding values; but this has very largely ceased to be so in the countries of the West.

Thus modern man is also much less prepared to accept any external trappings which simply cover up the Church's real nature. The Church is becoming increasingly obliged to give proof of its abiding values. By this I do not mean exclusively rational proof in the traditional sense, but the proof afforded by living faith. The external trappings belong here, because they are judged by whether they allow the inner values to shine through.

Basically, I think the Church is conscious of a need, even a theological need, to shape its mission in such a way that the inner values may become apparent to the world. I am thinking here, for example, of the Pope's gesture when he offered his tiara for the poor during the Council. This was relatively little in itself, and really nothing very special when one thinks of the Christian message. But what really strikes me as surprising is that the need for such a gesture has not been felt till now—at the eleventh hour, so to speak. And again, the fact that it was nothing more than a gesture which did not radically alter the face of the Curia.

Would you agree with me that a fundamental change in the external appearance of the Church might help make its witness more effective?

E. : If by a fundamental change in the external appearance of the Church you mean a renunciation of all visible expression of the Church's spiritual office I am unable to go along with you, for the reasons I have already given. Certainly I agree with you that prudence and bold determination alike are needed in changing any of the outer trappings which originated at a time when society itself was divided up hierarchically and each group had its own distinctive forms of apparel. These things have almost completely vanished. If the Church retains forms which social changes have rendered obsolete it only repels or estranges the outsiders and the lapsed, thus creating an additional impediment for its own pastoral work. As the discussions at the Council have shown, this realization is making more and more headway, especially since all these discussions about making the "aggiornamento" apply even to the external forms are based on the serious injunction of the gospel about humility and modesty as concerns the things of this world, which even went so far as to extol poverty as blessed—this injunction is making itself felt again. To my mind, one of the things which will give great impetus to our attempt to scrap outmoded forms will be the liturgical revival. This goes back to essentials and aims to bring them home to the people in the very heart of the Church's life—in the liturgy. The effects will certainly make themselves felt outside the liturgical sphere as well. But this is a time of mighty upheavals for everyone, the Church included; and we shall have to allow the Church a certain period of transition and not be too ungenerous in measuring it out.

c) *The striving for secular power*

M.: Another impression formed by many people about the Church points in the same direction, though its psychological effect is perhaps more serious. These people are of the opinion that the Church does not take its power from God or Christ but exclusively from the secular authorities. Without this it would have no power at all. The thought of the Church being without secular power has always been much dreaded, as a look at the Middle Ages will suffice to show. Nowadays, it is true, the Church allows itself to be supported by the secular authorities in a way different from that of the Middle Ages. Nonetheless, the danger is still there. Conditions in Spain, even if they are not quite so simple as some people like to make out, could serve as an example. Here in Germany our attention will be turned to the struggles over proportional representation for the denominations in politics and public institutions; not to mention the fear of the Church freeing itself from the state by collecting its necessary means of support direct from the faithful and not by way of the Inland Revenue.

Tendencies like these, which will obviously differ from country to country, will prejudice the authenticity of Christian witness in so far as any claim is laid to secular power in order to bolster up religious faith. This can perhaps be seen from the fact that the Church becomes much more credible in countries where it has to a very large extent to do without state assistance, as in the Communist countries. These tendencies, however briefly we have touched upon them here, have a lot to do with our theme of ideology, faith and conscience. The ideologist wants as much power as possible. As I have already suggested, he has a distorted grasp of things as they are, which makes his faith remote from reality; as a result he has to resort to power if he wants to propagate his faith. Moreover, since aggressive conscience is a distinctive mark of ideology, it plays a part here psychologically—though I do not wish to develop this point any further.

E.: The relation of the Church to secular power is and will always be a difficult and serious problem. You yourself are probably aware of the lively discussion which has been raised recently about whether the beginning of the "Constantinian era"—the mutual accommodation between the Church and the Roman state—really marked a sort of "fall from grace" on the part of the Church. The principles involved are too complicated to allow of any detailed examination in the discussion of our present theme. For this reason I will try only to clarify what seems to me important as regards the dangers to the credibility of the Church's witness.

Here, too, we shall have to be on our guard against oversimplification. It is not really permissible to claim that the only choice is between "faith without power and power without faith". The Church has always been faced with the temptation to use the secular authorities as a prop, and has often succumbed. But it cannot be maintained that it would ever have sacrificed its faith for the sake of secular power.

The problem will never allow of any complete solution, though there have obviously been many different attempts to solve it in terms of the historical situation; and it arises because the Catholic Church sees itself as a visible community, with a visible organization, visible laws and institutions, and so on. Consequently the *res mixtae*—that is to say, the matters in which the interests of eternal salvation and the secular state both coincide—suggest the desirability of agreements between Church and state. The forms this can take are historically conditioned. One thing, at least, is certain: the secularization of culture, with its emphasis on the autonomy of the state, and our modern pluralist society both exclude the possibility of the medieval solution with its use of the spiritual and temporal arms.

But it lies in the nature of things that any agreement between

Church and state involves state action in matters affecting the interests of the Church. Let us take, for example, the schools question or the marriage laws based on legislation or a concordat. There is nothing objectionable about this, and no reasonable person could claim that it destroys the authenticity of the Church's witness. It is another matter, of course, if the Church receives as a result of legislation or concordat a secular power to which it is no longer entitled in virtue of the real situation, such as the number of its "practising" members. But we have no intention of going into actual questions of the day; it will be enough to confine ourselves to the principles which have a direct bearing on our theme.

What seems to me even more important is that the Church must make it convincingly clear that it is not held in being as a result of any such agreements with the secular authorities, but through its faith and trust in the assistance promised to it by Christ.

I do not think it is a betrayal of the Church's legitimate interests to assert that not everything which might possibly be achieved by laws or concordats should necessarily be sought after or put into force. If use is made of the resources of secular power, then it should be governed by considerations of eternal salvation, and hence it may be necessary to take into account the possibility of damage being done to the Church's witness. This is probably all that need be said in this connection. I can only thank you for forcing the theologian to assess this question in pastoral terms, and not just as a theoretical exercise.

M.: The Church does seem to be sensing that it has not kept up with the times; in other words, it has certainly begun to notice that its preaching mission is being hindered by its cumbersomeness. This is clear from many recent efforts on the Church's part, and most evident among these efforts in the public eye have probably been the discussions and resolutions of the Council. But even outside the Council it is possible to see a number of attempts, among Catholics and Protestants alike, to bring Christ to the modern world.

All the same, not all these efforts seem to me to proceed from genuine faith, and for this reason they lack sufficient penetrating power. A number of them I would even consider superfluous, if not actually dangerous. They spring more from a desire to still the itch of conscience than from a creative impulse to make a personal experience of Christ visible to others. Here we could include everything which smacks more or less of advertising. One often gets the impression that the Church believes it can regain lost ground in the world by making its presence felt everywhere, on television, in the newspapers, out in the streets—and preferably with state help. To think that such measures can have lasting influence on personal religion seems to me illusory. What is more, they tend to distract attention from all the situations in which the Church has a real chance to show where its true centre lies and make its message credible to others.

E.: It is, of course, the Church's right and duty to advertise. It has been doing so ever since the times of the apostles and will continue to do so with all the contemporary means available. All the same, your comment strikes me as important. Not all and every form of advertising befits the nature and dignity of the Church. The Church's credibility is damaged by any advertising which is mere sales-talk rather than witness: when, for example, a person has reasons for feeling that gimmicks and smooth talk are being used to "bring him in" and to make him take a step to which he could not be brought by means of relevant examples, words and actions.

d) Sensitivity to concrete criticism

M.: At this point I should like to refer to a phenomenon which psychologically is highly relevant to the problem of authentic witness, because it leads the public to form the more or less unconscious impression that the preachers of Christian truth do not really take their inspiration from Christ. I am referring to the sensitivity of typical representatives of the Church to all criticism, however well disposed.

It is a phenomenon which psychotherapists encounter among people who will not acknowledge their guilt and are therefore unable to come to grips with it. That the official representatives of the Church—meaning first and foremost the priests— occasionally have a bad conscience about unacknowledged guilt can be demonstrated from many examples. For the psychotherapist the clearest indication perhaps is the Church's sensitivity to any concrete criticism. The Church reacts with great calmness and composure when guilt is imputed in general to one and all, since everybody's guilt is nobody's guilt; but as soon as it come to attacks aimed at some specific target there is great indignation. The best-known example in recent years is the reaction to Hochhuth's play, *The Representative*. I am not concerned here with whether Hochhuth was right or wrong in his criticism of Pius XII; what does concern me is the sensitive reaction, which went far beyond the bounds of rational assessment. Most striking of all is the fact that those who opposed Hochhuth simply took him up on futile points of detail and failed to see something with a very positive bearing for the Church. This positive element, to my mind, was the high moral valuation of the pope implicit in Hoch-huth's attacks. The very fact that more was being expected from a pope than from an ordinary priest, and that a pope was being measured up against the faith his Church proclaims, suggests a view of the papacy which would have been unthinkable half a century ago from anyone outside the Church. Or would the Church be more pleased to hear that nothing more can be expected from a pope than from anyone else? Yet within the Church itself the pope is declared to have a claim to a special hearing, whether his decisions are magisterial pronouncements or not—as you yourself emphasized at the beginning of our discussion. Many a priest has not hesitated to dismiss all implicit or explicit demands made on the pope as evidence of heresy, lèse-majesté or utopian thinking. You were saying earlier that the priest recites the Confiteor every day at Mass. Yet in the face of a daily acknowledgment of sin before God, the saints and one's fellow-men it cannot fail to strike any observer as rather odd that there should be such great sensitivity the moment some concrete deficiency is pointed out. All the more so since in the eyes of the Church guilt has eternal repercussions and is therefore to be taken very seriously indeed. In principle, then, the Church should be glad when its attention is drawn to guilt which has been overlooked or evaded; after all, the Church preaches Christ's observation that men are more inclined to see the speck in their brother's eye than the log in their own.

Psychotherapists are constantly dealing with repressed and unacknowledged guilt. Everyone tends to evade the issue with non-committal phrases; anything but honestly acknowledge some concrete piece of guilt. People will not accept criticisms of themselves; they pick holes in the critic. Every possible form of defence is mobilized. The Church itself does not hesitate to mobilize the state or its own rank-and-file, or to resort to unassailable theological arguments, in order to avoid admitting its own shortcomings. If this is not so, then why did Church circles find it so very special when the present Pope said: "If we share any blame for the schism in our faith, then we beg others for forgiveness."

I should like, then, to ask you whether you see this discrepancy between the acknowledgment of purely general guilt and the sensitivity to concrete criticism as a problem for moral theology, particularly as regards authenticity of witness?

E.: May I suggest that we leave Hochhuth's play aside? It is an unhappy example, because it is a shoddy work, of highly questionable historical value, as even non-Catholic and non-Christian critics have pointed out, and because it is extremely painful when someone belonging to a nation whose official representatives at that time had the murder of millions on their conscience, criticizes the silence of a man who was a particular friend of this nation and who, through his diplomatic relations with post-war Germany, was the first to help this country to take its place once more among the nations of the world.

I should like, then, to leave this example aside because it can only obscure the point you are making, and quite rightly—that the excessive sensitivity of the Church to criticisms of its life or its methods prejudices its credibility, since there is here a sign of what depth-psychology would call insecurity.

M.: All the same, I think the Hochhuth example can help throw light on a number of things under discussion here. Even if Hochhuth's criticisms over-simplify a complex historical matter and are much too one-sided, they have certainly helped to set the image of Pius XII free from the exaggerated eminence it quite unjustifiably enjoyed among many people both in and near the Church, and which he himself seems to have done much to foster. Why does it seem so impossible to admit, quite calmly, that the deliberations and actions of a pope, however well meant, may have fallen short of the moral standard called for at a time of mass atrocities? If the Church sees itself, among other things, as a Church of sinners it should surely be grateful to any critic who points out how it fails in practice and how far it falls short of the ideal it preaches.

And another thing. The hierarchy of the Church—and the higher it goes the worse this gets—is much too accustomed to judge and condemn. But it is another matter when the situation is reversed. Because the Church is conscious of possessing the truth it easily manoeuvres itself into a position where it will be only too likely to treat an attack upon itself as an attack upon the truth. On the occasions when it admits to some deficiency it comes up very quickly with excuses—excuses which are not given anything like so much prominence when the Church is condemning others and which are just as one-sided as Hochhuth's remarks.

This phenomenon can also be seen in connection with the underlying theme of our discussion: the relationship between ideology and faith. Ever since the Church became a world-wide institution it has assumed an increasing number of ideological features. This does not mean that every individual Catholic has an ideological faith; but when it comes to the Church's methods of propagating the faith we do quite frequently come across elements typical of ideology rather than of faith: missionary work with threats of violence ("baptism or the sword"), the condemnation of "deviationists", the maintenance of orthodoxy by the Inquisition with its frequently brutal methods, religion by secular decree ("*cuius regio, eius religio*") and plain bribery ("Paris is worth a Mass").

It would be possible to provide many more examples of the Church's proselytizing methods right down to the present day, and they would certainly show that the ideologizing of faith both has been and still is treated as something perfectly normal. This process is now being halted in the Christian world, as can be seen, among other things, from the growth in personal responsibility which you yourself have been emphasizing. But many bishops and priests will doubtless find this situation unfamiliar; they may give it their blessing intellectually, but they will have to adjust themselves to it emotionally as well.

E.: There is no point in trying to deny or dissimulate the fact that the religious dynamism of the Church as an historical institution is subject to fluctuation. The Church is, after all, human. There have certainly been periods when the Church's leaders have been afflicted by a greater measure of what can only be described as inner insecurity, even though it is possible to suggest extenuating circumstances, such as the defensive position the Church had to adopt for centuries towards the excessive emancipation of secular culture.

We will therefore be perfectly willing to accept as a guiding principle that whenever the Church reacts over-sensitively to criticism it would do well to examine the vitality and effectiveness of its religious faith in practice. Objectively, however, there are two factors to be taken into account. First: a psychotherapist who is convinced of the importance of psychotherapy will be much more ready to listen to criticism of his own person or professional activity than of psychotherapy in general, and in just the same way any honest representative of the Church will feel himself bound to stand up for his Church to the best of his ability, even though he may be quite prepared to answer for his own personal shortcomings. And secondly, it should not be forgotten that the Church is obliged to hold its ground against critics who are very much on the look-out for any ecclesiastical weaknesses or abuses, and who frequently misunderstand or distort the facts. With criticism at this level a measure of sensitivity is not only understandable but in many cases a duty. It is not a matter so much of upholding the Church's prestige; conversion or perseverance will only be made needlessly difficult for people who are unable to see through such machinations. And it remains to be seen in individual cases whether a conscientious acknowledgment of guilt will really be of help to anyone or whether it will simply be used by malicious opponents as a welcome new weapon against the Church. The example of the high-minded German Pope Hadrian VI is not exactly encouraging. A confession of weaknesses and failures which comes too lightly off the tongue can be just as prejudicial to the Church's credibility as any over-sensitivity to criticism. Instances of this in post-war Germany can offer food for thought.

Now that I have said all this I feel I can agree all the more readily with your principle that too much sensitivity towards criticism can endanger, or at least diminish, the credibility of those who preach the faith. Attempts to hush up failures, blunders or scandals enjoy only a very questionable success, as experience has shown, and they damage the Church more than a sincere willingness to face up to criticism and sift the wheat from the chaff—though this should be done preferably in the Church's own barn first. This applies to the ecclesiastical authorities; and even more important in our present context, it applies to individual representatives of the Church and even to all believing Christians in their dealings with non-Catholics. It is not only the Church's credibility in the eyes of the world which is at stake here but also, in many cases, the personal faith of the individual believer. Anyone who has the courage to face up to an unpleasant truth and, where necessary, to speak it out, is conscious of an inner liberation; and this will enable him to bear more joyful and effective witness to the truth which is Christ.

e) Lack of Christian charity

M.: There is one final point which, from my own experience, diminishes the power of Christian conviction in other people's eyes, and this is lack of love—a lack, in other words, of the virtue which Christian teaching presents as the supreme commandment. By love I do not mean the organized charity carried out extensively by the Church. Nor am I referring to the help which many priests render here and there, often at the cost of great sacrifices. I am referring to the love which I tried to define at the beginning: an ability to respond fully to another person. Love of neighbour, as a general requirement, depends on the stage of development reached by the human race, and it is necessary to be constantly thinking it out anew and finding new ways of putting it into practice. The general development at present seems to suggest that closer individual attention should be given to the needs of soul and spirit rather than to material requirements. Christian charity, in other words, is moving more towards the sphere of personal relationships.

This aspect of charity brings to my mind the widespread complaints of patients, Christians and non-Christians alike, about the inability of priests to deal with individuals for their own sake. These people feel they are not understood, and that their real needs are overlooked. They are consoled with biblical texts and suggested reading-matter, or with purely general principles, none of which touches their own personal existence. Principles, after all, can set up barriers to communication. This has been remarked on for years, and it is one of the reasons why modern man has turned from the priest to the psychotherapist.

One of the first reactions might be to put the blame on celibacy, which has, in fact, been done. If this turned out to be true it would contradict one of the reasons put forward for celibacy, which is that a celibate priest has more freedom to devote himself to Christ and the service of the Christian community. In practice, celibate priests probably do not, on the whole, do any more for their parishioners than the married Protestant clergy, or than a union official for his union. But this impression may be deceptive.

I myself am inclined to think that the lack of immediacy in Christian love is not to be attributed to celibacy—not primarily, at least. My guess is confirmed by the growing number of enquiries concerned with Protestant pastors or Communist functionaries. Here, too, there is evidence of a lack of personal closeness even with one's nearest and dearest wherever those in question have the ideological mentality. The marriages of such people are more strongly marked by devotion to an idea, or to humanity as a whole, or to the future, than by an immediate concern for the needs of wife and children as individuals. I outlined all this in my model example.

If these guesses are confirmed over a wider range of individual cases it will mean that many priests are not blind to the individual needs of others because they are celibate, but that they remain celibate because they are unconsciously shut in on themselves.

The examination of this problem finds support even in ecclesiastical quarters—but whatever the pattern of motivation behind a priest's choice of vocation may be, lack of love is something which takes a lot of force out of the Christian message of love. Priests like this are ideological functionaries rather than chosen people who have known the Lord for themselves.

E.: We priests, too, are children of our times. This means that we will fail, and then excuse ourselves; for we do not remain unaffected by the modern trend to collectivize and manipulate humanity. As a result, our personal response to our fellow-men will suffer, and we will all too easily refer them and their needs to the appropriate "machinery".

The Church is aware of the fatal danger which this disregard for persons represents for the world, and it is trying to counter it within its own sphere of influence. But the Church's representatives will still succumb, especially when they are overburdened with work. That is the long and the short of it.

All I can say, then, is that we must do our best, both in general and in particular, to take very seriously the claim made upon us by the New Testament when it talks of our "neighbour": that we should be ready to give our personal love and attention to any man whom God puts in our path. To be open to everyone at all times is an almost super-human demand; but we must persevere, even when we realize that we have just missed an opportunity and will probably miss another before much time has gone by. The priest, too, finds it difficult today to be a Christian.

You are quite right in saying that celibacy is not in itself a hindrance any more than marriage is in itself a help; both depend on mature decision. The pastoral priest—whether in training or, technically at least, fully qualified—is faced first of all with a duty which the Church is coming to realize more clearly than before: that more must be cultivated than a few selected virtues highly prized in ecclesiastical surroundings. Justice must be done to all the essential aspects of life; a priest must experience them for himself and arrive at a personal response. And again you are right: where this does not happen and a person remains more or less shut in on himself, then a decision for celibacy, and for the priesthood, will have been a false one.

But even this is not enough. Love of neighbour is a question of faith. Genuine faith means that a Christian must say "yes" to Christ as regards his own person and the whole of his life; it means not only that he accepts the whole of revealed truth but also that he allows his life to be modelled on God's Word. But a Christian who lacks this faith will never be able to respond to others in their uniqueness as individual persons, and he will not recognize their needs as a call coming to him from God. In this sense, love of our neighbour is indeed the hardest test of faith. If it is missing, the credibility of Christian witness will be reduced to a minimum—in our own times especially.

Love comes from faith, and faith comes from what is heard. This is what determines the credibility or otherwise of those whose vocation it is to preach the faith. Every priest is called, inspired and ultimately judged by Christ, who lived among us "as one who serves" (*Luke* 22:27).